100 MUST-TRY NEW ZEALAND WINES

MICHAEL COOPER

PHOTOGRAPHS BY SIMON YOUNG

Hodder Moa

National Library of New Zealand Cataloguing-in-Publication Data

Cooper, Michael, 1952-

100 must-try New Zealand wines / Michael Cooper.

Includes index.

ISBN 978-1-86971-217-4

1. Wine and wine making—New Zealand—Handbooks, manuals, etc.

2. Wine—Purchasing—New Zealand—Handbooks, manuals, etc.

I. Title.

641.2202993—dc 22

A Hodder Moa Book

Published in 2011 by Hachette New Zealand Ltd

4 Whetu Place, Mairangi Bay

Auckland, New Zealand

www.hachette.co.nz

Designed and produced by Hachette New Zealand Ltd

Printed by Everbest Printing Co Ltd, China

CONTENTS

PREFACE

This is not a comprehensive, technical or 'serious' book on New Zealand wine. It was fun to plan, fun to write — and the wines were certainly fun to taste.

The whole idea of the book is to give you a diverse and stimulating array of New Zealand wines to choose from, regardless of whether you are in the mood for a wine of sublime quality, or looking for something new and exciting, or just thirsting for a bargain.

Many of the wines are featured because they rank among the country's greatest. Others are included because, from one vintage to the next, they offer irresistible value.

Still others provide an intriguing glimpse of possible future directions for New Zealand wine. These are the single profiles of wines made from grape varieties relatively new to this country, such as Verdelho, Arneis, Grüner Veltliner, Montepulciano and Tempranillo.

Some of New Zealand's greatest wines are not represented in these pages. A regularly revised list of New Zealand's wine classics can be found in my annual *Buyer's Guide to New Zealand Wines*. And some of the text for this book has been updated from my book *Classic Wines of New Zealand* (second edition 2005).

You *will* find many of the top wines here. You will also discover some wonderful buys and suggestions of rare new varieties, worth tracking down.

Around the world, interest is growing in organic wines. Three of the wines featured here have been certified by BioGro and are identified as 'Certified Organic'.

The basic goal was to highlight 100 New Zealand wines of special interest and provide something for all readers, regardless of their taste preferences and budgets.

I hope this book leads you to some great discoveries.

Michael Cooper

THE VARIETIES

Arneis

See page 102

Chardonnay

From the Karikari Peninsula in Northland to Alexandra in Central Otago, New Zealand produces well over 500 Chardonnays. Although less popular here than Sauvignon Blanc, Chardonnay is still recognised internationally as the greatest of all grapes for dry white wine. New Zealand's Chardonnays are grown up to 1200 kilometres apart, so it's no surprise the wines display intriguing regional differences.

Three regions dominate production. Hawke's Bay is renowned for sturdy Chardonnays with rich, ripe grapefruit and stone-fruit flavours, finely balanced acidity and the ability to mature well. Gisborne's greatest asset is the enormous drink-young charm of its softly mouthfilling Chardonnays. Those from Marlborough are slightly leaner and crisper in their youth, but can flourish with cellaring.

Sauvignon Blanc and Pinot Gris are usually made entirely in stainless steel tanks, placing their accents on fresh, vibrant fruit flavours. But unoaked Chardonnay can easily be boring. Chardonnay is not highly aromatic and its varietal flavours are more restrained than those of Sauvignon Blanc. A gentle seasoning of oak, which adds richness and complexity but does not overpower the subtle fruit flavours, simply makes Chardonnay more interesting and enjoyable.

New Zealand's top Chardonnays are all fermented and matured in barrels, usually 225-litre French oak barriques. The result is a more satisfying, rich and multi-faceted wine, with extra layers of flavour.
See pages 20, 22, 26, 28, 40, 50, 62, 68, 72, 82, 88, 92, 94, 98, 116

Chenin Blanc

See page 66

Gewürztraminer

Some popular white wines — Chardonnay, Pinot Gris — have restrained, subtle flavours that enhance a wide range of dishes and occasions. We drink them anytime. Gewürztraminer is the ultimate 'mood' wine. A hedonist's delight, it's a wine to broach occasionally with an Indian curry, or when you are simply in the mood to delight in its rich spiciness and overwhelming perfume.

If you struggle to pronounce the name of this once-tried, never-forgotten variety, join the group. Rather than ask for a bottle of 'Ge-vertz-truh-mean-ah', most wine lovers just call it 'Ge-vertz', which means spicy. Of the adjectives used in relation to the most distinctive and pungent white-wine variety of all, 'spicy' is the most common, but many tasters are also reminded of cinnamon, lychees, cloves, gingerbread, mangoes, mint and freshly ground black pepper.

In Alsace, Gewürztraminer yields striking wines — sturdy, lush and ravishingly scented. New Zealand's Gewürztraminers have attracted international praise (Matawhero winery, in Gisborne, claimed in 1999 that its Gewürztraminer was 'served at the Queen's table and is reputed to be one of her favourite wines'), but few can stand close comparison with the benchmark wines of Alsace.

First planted here over a century ago, Gewürztraminer still accounts for just one per cent of the national vineyard. The vines are clustered in Gisborne, Marlborough and Hawke's Bay, with smaller pockets in Nelson and Central Otago.

For the wine industry's accountants, Gewürztraminer is a grape to be avoided or restricted to a small plot. Although it ripens easily, it is susceptible to poor weather at flowering, which can dramatically reduce the crop.

Fine-quality Gewürztraminers can mature gracefully for several years,

but the best are so gloriously fragrant, flavour-packed and well-rounded in
their youth that cellaring is an option, rather than a necessity.
See pages 60, 64, 86, 120

Grüner Veltliner

See page 38

Malbec

See page 218

Merlot, Cabernet Sauvignon & Blends

Cabernet Sauvignon and Merlot are the greatest varieties in the world's
greatest red-wine region — Bordeaux. Merlot and Cabernet Sauvignon are
also the foundation of many of New Zealand's richest, most complex and
long-lived reds, especially those from Hawke's Bay and Waiheke Island.

Everywhere in Bordeaux, except in the Médoc and Graves districts,
Merlot is more widely planted than Cabernet Sauvignon. In New Zealand,
Merlot's key attraction is that it ripens 10 days to two weeks earlier than
Cabernet Sauvignon, and is thus capable of achieving higher sugar levels,
lower acidity and riper fruit flavours. The grapes are used in Cabernet
Sauvignon-predominant blends, but the majority are reserved for straight
varietal Merlots and Merlot-based blends.

Cabernet Sauvignon once dominated New Zealand's red-wine
production, but is now less prominent than Pinot Noir, Merlot and even
Syrah. Don't underestimate this exceptional grape variety. Here, it performs
best at warm, free-draining inland sites in Hawke's Bay (Gimblett Gravels
and the Havelock North hills) and on north-facing slopes on Waiheke Island,
yielding sturdy wine of a fragrance, delicacy and depth that can be distinctly
reminiscent of a fine Bordeaux.

Many leading reds are Merlot/Cabernet Sauvignon or Cabernet
Sauvignon/Merlot blends, in which the Merlot adds its lush fruit flavours

and velvety mouthfeel to the more angular, slowly evolving Cabernet Sauvignon. Other classic grapes of Bordeaux (Cabernet Franc, Malbec, Petit Verdot, Carmenère) are also blended with Merlot and Cabernet Sauvignon, adding to the complexity of the country's finest claret-style reds.

See pages 152, 160, 162, 164, 166, 174, 176, 202, 212, 214, 216, 220, 222, 226, 230, 232, 234

Montepulciano

See page 186

Pinot Blanc

See page 52

Pinotage

See page 192

Pinot Gris

The runaway popularity of Pinot Gris in New Zealand shows no signs of abating. Some Marlborough grape-growers, no longer able to sell their Sauvignon Blanc or Pinot Noir crops, have recently replaced their vines with Pinot Gris. Over 300 Pinot Gris are now crowding the shelves.

Plantings of the traditional Alsace variety have soared from 130 hectares of bearing vines in 2000 to 1725 hectares in 2011. Pinot Gris is now New Zealand's third most widely planted white-wine variety, trailing only Sauvignon Blanc and Chardonnay.

Exports have risen tenfold over the last five years and now exceed 300,000 cases. With Pinot Gris — as with Sauvignon Blanc and Pinot Noir — winemakers have discovered a classic variety that, overall, performs better here than in Australia.

Wine marketer David Nicholas has pointed out that Pinot Gris 'appeared on the market at the right time to pick up the ABC (Anything But

Chardonnay) consumers'. Pinot Gris even has some Chardonnay-like traits — mouthfilling body, gentle acidity and peachy, non-aggressive flavours.

The problem is that Pinot Gris can easily be boring. Some winemakers see Pinot Gris as 'like working with white paint on a white background'. A key issue is that Pinot Gris has a tendency to over-crop, yielding unripe, dilute wines. Small crops are needed to build the concentrated, ripe stone-fruit and spice flavours of fine Pinot Gris.

The six Pinot Gris featured in this book include four of New Zealand's most striking Pinot Gris and two compelling bargains.

See pages 24, 42, 54, 96, 118, 124

Pinot Noir

Pinot Noir triggers a more emotional response from wine drinkers than any other variety. One New Zealand producer enthuses that their vineyard is 'where beautiful wines are created, with what is best for the land, the grape and the soul. For us, it is the relentless pursuit of creating great enjoyment, wrapped in mystery, with a touch of sensuality. Wine caressed by angels.'

Why is Pinot Noir — the classic grape of Burgundy — so popular? A key factor is its easy-drinking nature, based on its ripe sweet-fruit flavours and gentle tannins. Some reds are powerful but austere in their youth, needing years to mellow and reveal their greatness, but Pinot Noir can knock your socks off within a couple of years of the harvest.

Pinot Noir thrives in cool climates, where its grapes can hang on the vines for extended periods, picking up the most subtle scents and flavours. The majority of Pinot Noir vines in New Zealand are found from the Wairarapa south, in regions characterised by cold night temperatures and relatively low autumn rainfall.

Distinct regional styles have emerged, ranging from Martinborough's sturdy, warm and savoury reds to Central Otago's notably perfumed and supple, instantly appealing Pinot Noirs. Marlborough's top labels are widely underrated.

See pages 154, 156, 158, 170, 172, 178, 182, 184, 188, 196, 200, 206, 208, 224, 236

Riesling

Every summer, we visit friends on Auckland's west coast. Sharpening our appetites in the surf, we later relax on their deck overlooking the ocean and enjoy lunch — and a gently chilled bottle of Riesling.

When summer's heat descends, you need cool, vibrant, appetisingly crisp wines that will revive and refresh you. A garden-fresh, racy Riesling is a stimulating apéritif. And with typical summer fare, such as fish, cold chicken and salads, an invitingly scented, light and tangy Riesling can be hard to resist.

Far behind Sauvignon Blanc and Chardonnay, and overtaken by Pinot Gris, Riesling is New Zealand's fourth most widely planted white-wine grape. A classic 'cool-climate' variety, it is well suited to the South Island's cooler growing temperatures and lower humidity. Its stronghold is Marlborough, but the grape is also planted extensively in Nelson, Canterbury and Central Otago.

Rieslings range from bone-dry to unabashedly sweet, and that versatility is a strength and a weakness. There's a Riesling style to suit most drinkers, but those who inadvertently buy a sweet wine when expecting something dry, or vice versa, can be put off. Most New Zealand Rieslings are medium-bodied (11 to 13 per cent alcohol), with a sliver of sweetness to balance their lively acidity. See pages 46, 56, 78, 80, 110, 122

Rosé

See page 148

Sauvignon Blanc

Sauvignon Blanc (or more precisely, Marlborough Sauvignon Blanc) is *the* classic wine style of New Zealand, in the eyes of the world. When Ross and Bill Spence of Matua Valley made New Zealand's first Sauvignon Blanc in 1974, who could have foreseen what lay ahead?

Marlborough is New Zealand's — some say the world's — Sauvignon Blanc capital. Over 85 per cent of the country's vines are in Marlborough, where Sauvignon Blanc accounts for 75 per cent of all plantings. With their

leap-out-of-the-glass, ripely herbaceous aromas and pungent, garden-fresh flavours, the Sauvignon Blancs here can be of breathtaking intensity.

Sauvignon Blanc's assertive grassy notes in New Zealand stem from a high concentration in the grapes of an organic compound that is much easier to drink than it is to pronounce — methoxypyrazine. The variety's green capsicum-like flavours (well-ripened examples also display tropical-fruit characters, such as passionfruit and pineapple) are not flattered by oak, and in fact most New Zealand Sauvignon Blancs are cool-fermented in stainless steel tanks, placing their accent squarely on their fresh, assertive varietal flavours.

However, for many of the best wines, oak is part of the recipe. A minor part of the blend (5 to 10 per cent) is fermented in seasoned — rather than new — French oak casks, to add a subtle extra dimension.

See pages 30, 32, 34, 36, 58, 70, 76, 84, 90, 104, 108, 114

Sparkling Wine

New Zealand's finest fizz is made by the classic technique called *méthode traditionnelle*, in which the second, bubble-creating fermentation takes place not in a tank, like cheaper wines, but in the bottle itself, as in Champagne (the real stuff, from the world's most famous wine region).

During the wine's lengthy maturation in the bottle (anything from nine months to three years, but typically 18 months to two years) the yeast cells gradually decompose, conferring distinctive, bready, yeasty characters on the wine that add greatly to its complexity and richness.

The quality of a fine sparkling wine also reflects the standard of its base wine. Pinot Noir and Chardonnay, both varieties of pivotal importance in Champagne, are the foundations of New Zealand's top bubblies. Most of the best wines flow from Marlborough, where the incisive fruit flavours and tense acidity have attracted not only locally owned producers but several overseas-controlled companies.

See pages 134–145

Sweet Wine

The finest of New Zealand's sweet white wines are world class. For instance, Seifried Winemakers Collection Sweet Agnes Riesling Ice Wine 2008 won the trophy for 'Best Sweet White Over Ten Pounds' at the 2009 *Decanter* World Wine Awards, judged in London.

Riesling is the key grape, yielding ravishingly perfumed wines with concentrated varietal flavours to which 'noble rot', the desirable form of *Botrytis cinerea* fungus, adds a honeyed, apricot-like richness. Marlborough has so far been the source of the majority of the greatest sweet Rieslings, but outstanding dessert wines are also flowing from several other regions and varieties, including Gewürztraminer, Pinot Gris, Chardonnay, Sauvignon Blanc and Chenin Blanc.

Also well worth discovering are the weighty, complex dessert wines from Hawke's Bay. Typically barrel-aged, in the past they were mostly based on Sémillon, but recently Viognier has also come to the fore.

See pages 128–131

Syrah

Who makes the best Syrah: Australia (where they call it Shiraz) or New Zealand? That's like asking which region produces the finest Sauvignon Blanc: Marlborough or the Barossa Valley?

Or is it? Hawke's Bay and Waiheke Island have a hot new red-wine grape variety. There are now over 150 New Zealand Syrahs on the shelves and the country has 300 hectares of bearing Syrah vines — a steep rise from 62 hectares in 2000.

Syrah, the traditional black grape of the Rhône Valley, is now spread widely through the south of France. It is also Australia's most widely planted red-wine grape. New Zealand was long seen as too cool for this late-ripening variety, but the wines that have emerged over the past decade have been unexpectedly classy.

Regardless of the name of the vine or the location of the vineyard, Syrah typically yields robust, richly flavoured reds with a heady perfume. Top versions are almost opaque, with a characteristic spicy, black-pepper aroma and flavour.

So who makes the best wine, Australia or New Zealand? Let's just enjoy their difference. The style of New Zealand Syrah is more akin to the floral, elegant, finely structured reds of the Rhône Valley than the power-packed, often jammy and sweetly oaked style common in Australia.

See pages 168, 190, 194, 198, 204

Tempranillo

See page 228

Verdelho

See page 44

Viognier

See pages 106, 112

WHITE

ATA RANGI CRAIGHALL CHARDONNAY

>>> '**SEAMLESS**' is a word that crops up again and again in my tasting notes for this celebrated Martinborough Chardonnay. Powerful and lush, with highly concentrated, peachy, nutty flavours and a deliciously rich, smooth finish, it's one of New Zealand's most opulent Chardonnays, skilfully balanced and very harmonious.

The partners in Ata Rangi — Clive Paton, Phyll Pattie and Alison Paton — look to classic white Burgundy for their inspiration, but are not trying to emulate its style. 'Our wine will always have greater fruit character. But many New Zealand Chardonnays have obvious oak influence, or obvious "malo" [buttery, creamy notes from a secondary, softening malolactic fermentation]. We're aiming for that seamless character, the integration that fine white Burgundy shows — that's the mentality that runs right through our approach.'

Price: **$38**

The sheltered, gently sloping Craighall Vineyard lies directly opposite Ata Rangi's Home Block and winery in Puruatanga Road, on the eastern edge of the Martinborough Terrace. Planted in a shallow layer of silt loams over alluvial gravels, the 1.8 hectares of irrigated Chardonnay vines are all of the Mendoza clone, which gives very low yields (averaging 4 tonnes of hand-picked grapes per hectare). The age of the ungrafted vines (25 years in

2011) is also giving fruit 'weight', which 'sucks up the oak'.

In the winery, the juice is not clarified by settling before the ferment (to impart a 'solids' character to the wine). Fermentation is with natural yeasts in Burgundy oak barriques (25 per cent new). The wine is then matured on its lees in the casks, with lees-stirring to enhance its complexity and 'vinosity' (the distinctive body and flavour of wine), for about 10 months.

The result is a wine with great presence in the mouth. Its notably concentrated, ripe-fruit characters give drink-young appeal, but the wine also possesses the power and structure to mature well for several years.

Ata Rangi Craighall Chardonnay is no longer entered in competitions, but the partners say they get their greatest satisfaction from their customers, 'who contact us to say how well their cellared bottles are drinking'.

From a vineyard south of Masterton, in the northern Wairarapa, the winery also produces a lower-priced wine, Ata Rangi Petrie Chardonnay ($28). Fragrant, rich and creamy, it typically has sweet-fruit flavours, a distinct touch of butterscotch and a well-rounded finish.

A classy wine in its own right, you could call it a junior Craighall.

If you like this wine, also try: Ata Rangi Petrie Chardonnay; Mission Jewelstone Hawke's Bay Chardonnay

BABICH IRONGATE CHARDONNAY

>>>

WHEN Joe Babich made the first Irongate Chardonnay in 1985, he told no one — not even his brother and partner, Peter. 'I was making it in a French style, and kept it a secret in case it was a failure,' recalls Joe. 'I used to furtively stir the barrels after work, when nobody was around.'

Irongate is one of New Zealand's most subtle, classically proportioned and long-lived Chardonnays. Although far from a blockbuster style, show success was swift. The 1985 won a gold medal and the Vintners Trophy for the best current vintage dry white at the 1985 National Wine Competition, a feat repeated in 1987. Babich's white-wine flagship, it remains a classy, distinctive wine that often performs outstandingly in the cellar.

Price: **$33**

What is the style goal? 'The vineyard [in Gimblett Road, in the heart of the Gimblett Gravels district of Hawke's Bay] delivers focused, steely, rich, intensely flavoured Chardonnay,' says winemaker Adam Hazeldine. 'We aim to reveal and embellish this with the gentle use of oak, lees-stirring and minimal fining. At all costs, we wish to avoid distracting the taster with excessive oak or malolactic [fermentation] influence.'

The past decade has brought some production changes, including a move to lower crops, hand-picking, fermentation with natural yeasts and a limited amount of malolactic fermentation, if required. 'We are aiming to make the wine richer and softer, while retaining its steely focus, longevity and personality,' says Hazeldine.

Joe Babich — for many years the winemaker and a senior wine judge, now the company's managing director — has 'never been a fan of blowsy, excessively woody Chardonnay that tastes good for 18 months and then falls away. My goal with Irongate Chardonnay has been to create a wine that in style fits between the flintiness of Chablis and the opulence of Montrachet.'

Named after an aquifer flowing under the Gimblett Gravels, Irongate is a single-vineyard wine. The vines, grown in extremely free-draining soils, develop small, open canopies of foliage, facilitating the grapes' exposure to the sun. Crops are limited to 6 tonnes of grapes per hectare, all hand-picked.

In the winery, the juice is fermented with natural yeasts in French oak barriques (25 per cent new). The wine, lees-aged and lees-stirred for up to 11 months, is bottled dry, with an alcohol content of 13 to 14.5 per cent, and then bottle-aged for a further year prior to its release.

Irongate makes a distinctive statement. In past vintages intense, lean and flinty, it is still far from being fat or creamy-soft, although today it offers more drink-young charm. It remains a very graceful wine, revealing great delicacy and finesse.

If you like this wine, also try: Sacred Hill Riflemans Chardonnay; Spy Valley Envoy Marlborough Chardonnay

BLACKENBROOK VINEYARD NELSON PINOT GRIS

>>> DANIEL Schwarzenbach has long yearned to make a great Pinot Gris. 'Before starting our own vineyard, I worked as a cellar hand for Domaine Zind-Humbrecht in Alsace, one of the top Pinot Gris producers worldwide. It was a fantastic experience and I couldn't wait to get home and start planting. . .'

Today, in the rolling Moutere hill country, only 500 metres from the coast,

Price: **$27**

Daniel and his wife, Ursula, produce one of this country's most striking Pinot Gris. In the classic Alsace mould, it is a powerful, high-alcohol wine, enticingly floral, with a strong surge of peach, pear and spice flavours, hints of apple strudel and honey, gentle sweetness, and lovely vibrancy and richness.

Blackenbrook has a strong reputation for 'aromatic' white wines — not just Pinot Gris, but also Riesling, Gewürztraminer and Muscat. Schwarzenbach (whose name translates as Blackenbrook) was born in Switzerland and came to New Zealand as a nine-year-old in 1975. After working as a medical technologist, he changed tack, gained a postgraduate diploma in viticulture and oenology from Lincoln University — then plunged into winemaking in Europe.

Schwarzenbach worked at respected estates in

Austria, Germany and Switzerland (Weingut Georg Fromm — who then also owned the acclaimed Marlborough winery that still bears his name), and in 1997 arrived at Domaine Zind-Humbrecht. There, he worked with the legendary Olivier Humbrecht, who became, says Daniel, his 'role model, in many respects'.

Humbrecht is no follower of convention, says Schwarzenbach. 'If it doesn't make sense in his view, he'll find a different solution that is simpler, gentler, better for the environment and obviously better for the vines and wines.' In the 8-hectare Blackenbrook Vineyard, on a gentle, north-facing slope, mussel shells are mulched to encourage earthworms. The gravity-fed winery, dug partly into a clay bank, facilitates minimal pumping of the juice and wine.

Harvested by hand at a very advanced stage of ripening (about 25 brix), the estate-grown Pinot Gris is cool-fermented in stainless steel tanks. The ferment is arrested to leave a touch of residual sugar in the wine, creating a medium-dry style.

Blackenbrook Vineyard Nelson Pinot Gris 2008 won the trophy for champion Pinot Gris at that year's New Zealand International Wine Show. Every vintage, I describe it as 'a distinctly Alsace-style wine'.

Olivier Humbrecht would probably be impressed too.

If you like this wine, also try: Blackenbrook Vineyard Nelson Gewürztraminer; Waimea Nelson Pinot Gris

CHURCH ROAD HAWKE'S BAY CHARDONNAY

AT its average retail price in supermarkets of $15, this is an irresistible bargain. Although made in large volumes, it is still a classy wine, mouthfilling, with concentrated, ripe stone-fruit flavours, nutty, biscuity notes adding complexity, and a creamy-smooth finish. It's a match for many producers' $25 or $30 Chardonnays.

Chardonnay is just one of this historic winery's achievements. A Mecca for tourists, Church Road lies at the foot of the Taradale Hills in Hawke's Bay. Apart from an underground wine museum and the atmospheric Tom McDonald Cellar — used for cultural events and winemakers' dinners — the winery boasts a popular restaurant, hosts outdoor concerts and produces outstanding white and red wines.

Price: $14–27

The winery was founded in 1896 by Bartholomew Steinmetz, a lay brother at the adjacent Marist Mission — now Mission Estate Winery. The story goes that after falling in love, Luxembourg-born Steinmetz left the mission and planted his own 2-hectare plot, producing his first vintage at Taradale Vineyards in 1901.

After Montana (now Pernod Ricard NZ) snapped up the old winery in the late 1980s, the first vintage of Church Road flowed in 1990. Over the past 22 vintages, the Chardonnays have evolved from an emphasis on fresh fruit flavours seasoned with obvious, toasty oak to a less 'fruit-driven', less woody, more subtle and harmonious style. Lessons learned from the small-volume Church Road Cuve Chardonnay, developed to explore traditional Burgundian techniques, have flowed through to the less upfront, increasingly elegant Church Road Reserve Chardonnay and now to this 'standard' Chardonnay.

Most of the company's Chardonnay vineyards grow in river valleys, in close proximity to calcareous hillsides. The river sediments include silt, sand and gravel, while outwash from the hills introduces clay, which helps to produce Chardonnay 'with substance, fragrance and complexity'.

At the winery, 'we focus on getting the juice away from the skins as quickly as possible and encourage oxidation to give a softer, gentler palate structure,' says senior winemaker Chris Scott, who has worked at Church Road since 1998. Much of the wine undergoes a secondary, softening malolactic fermentation. The juice is fermented in French (70 per cent) and Hungarian (30 per cent) oak barriques (about one-third new), and the wine is matured for about 10 months on its yeast lees (sediment), which are stirred fortnightly, imparting a nutty, mealy aroma.

Fleshy and rounded, with substantial body and ripe, peachy flavours showing very good texture, complexity and depth, Church Road Hawke's Bay Chardonnay is a deservedly popular wine. Church Road is also the source of an equally great-value Merlot/Cabernet Sauvignon (see page 160).

BEST BUY

If you like this wine, also try: Church Road Reserve Hawke's Bay Chardonnay; Stoneleigh Marlborough Chardonnay

CLOS de STE ANNE CHARDONNAY NABOTH'S VINEYARD

CLOS de Ste Anne is the 'ultra-premium' label of The Millton Vineyard at Gisborne. It appears on this arrestingly rich, slowly evolving Chardonnay — but what does the brand mean?

'Clos is French for enclosure,' says James Millton, Gisborne's best-known winemaker. 'In wine terms, "clos" relates to wines made from an individual vineyard. 'Ste' offers a degree of feminine reverence and appreciation, with reference to 1 Kings Chapter 21 in the Old Testament. 'Anne' is the tribute I give to Annie [his wife and partner in the winery], for the support and understanding required to produce a fine bottle of wine.'

Price: $54

Gisborne built its reputation on fruity, ripe, rounded Chardonnays, full of drink-young charm. Millton Gisborne Chardonnay Riverpoint Vineyard and the more oak-influenced Millton Gisborne Chardonnay Opou Vineyard are both classic examples of the style, but the Clos de Ste Anne Chardonnay is a different beast, placing its accent on tightness, minerality and longevity.

'The wine has some softness and richness,' says Millton, 'but I want it to have a calcified minerality and purity of flavour and finish. As the vineyard gets older, like us, the wine is becoming more polished and complex.' He describes Clos de Ste Anne Chardonnay as 'a delicate and subtle food wine with hints of grilled bread, honey and cloves on the nose . . . [and] a pure, crisp mineral flavour.'

The grapes are sourced exclusively from Naboth's Vineyard at Manutuke, a steep, 2-hectare block with a commanding view across the Poverty Bay flats to the coast. The soils are shallow volcanic loams, overlying sedimentary limestone and sandstone. Pronounced 'Nay-both' (rhyming with cloth), the vineyard was planted with Chardonnay and Pinot Noir in 1989.

Designed for cellaring, Clos de Ste Chardonnay is based on very low-yielding (3.5 tonnes of grapes per hectare, on average), unirrigated vines. Hand-picked, it is barrel-fermented with natural yeasts, but malolactic fermentation is normally avoided, to underline its pure, crisp, minerally personality. Rather than new barrels, the more 'discreet' influence of second-fill French oak casks is preferred.

A very powerful, complex wine, with tight, citrusy, minerally flavours, Clos de Ste Anne Chardonnay typically drinks superbly at three to five years old, but matures very gracefully for a decade, becoming softer, more toasty and honeyed with age.

If you like this wine, also try: Craggy Range Les Beaux Cailloux; Millton Gisborne Chardonnay Opou Vineyard

CLOS HENRI MARLBOROUGH SAUVIGNON BLANC

>>> HOW'S this for flattery? Domaine Henri Bourgeois, the producer of some of France's top Sauvignon Blancs, expanded into Marlborough in 2001, establishing Clos Henri, inland from Renwick. 'Our ultimate objective is to offer a wine that tells you the story of its origins, whispers it's not French but from Marlborough, and voices that it is crafted from the specific Clos Henri *terroir*,' says the head of the family, Jean-Marie Bourgeois.

Price: $29

Clos Henri is a notably ripe style of Sauvignon Blanc with rich tropical-fruit flavours and a minerally thread. Fresh, punchy and dry, it shows excellent depth, complexity and roundness. A sophisticated wine, in top vintages it's a joy to drink.

Henri Bourgeois, a big company with extensive vineyards in Sancerre and Pouilly-Fumé, was founded in 1952 by Etienne Henri Bourgeois, a descendant of many generations of Sancerre wine-growers. Clos Henri is not 'simply after a herbaceous quality,' says Jean-Marie. 'Rather, we want Sauvignon Blanc to show roundness, richness, texture — all the attributes we associate with fine wine.'

On a hill site and flat land, Sauvignon Blanc and Pinot Noir are close-planted in a mix of stony riverbed soils (75 per cent) and clays (25 per cent.)

By 2012, when planting is scheduled to finish, the estate vineyard will cover 65 hectares.

Winemaker Damien Yvon, who grew up in the Loire Valley, told UK writer Rosemary George, in *Decanter* magazine, that 'the Bourgeois family is not keen on varietal character. You must control the vigour, and pick when everything is ripe, to avoid greenness.'

The grapes are hand-harvested from low-cropped vines (7 tonnes per hectare) cultivated in gravelly soils. The juice is fermented in a mix of stainless steel tanks (90 per cent) and old French oak puncheons (10 per cent), and then matured on its light yeast lees, with regular stirring, for up to 10 months.

Here's how Clos Henri describes the wine: 'The nose shows finesse and restraint — subtle aromas of peach, lime and coconut, supported by a nice minerality. The mouth follows the nose, with roundness and mouthfeel; the wine also stands out by a present, but not overwhelming, acidity. The mouth is long and the minerality persists.'

If you are looking for a deliciously easy-drinking style of Sauvignon Blanc, rich, ripe and well-rounded, Clos Henri is for you. Grown in clay — rather than stony — soils, Bel Echo by Clos Henri Sauvignon Blanc is slightly less rich, but still satisfying. So, too, is the lowest-priced Sauvignon Blanc of the trio, Petit Clos by Clos Henri, based on young vines.

If you like this wine, also try: Bel Echo by Clos Henri Marlborough Sauvignon Blanc; Seresin Marlborough Sauvignon Blanc

CLOS MARGUERITE MARLBOROUGH SAUVIGNON BLANC

'WE probably are control freaks,' admits Marguerite Van Hove. 'We don't use contract labour; we don't use contract grapes; we don't use contract winemaking. Our view has always been to build a business around things we own and control.'

Since the first vintage in 2002, Clos Marguerite has stood out as one of the region's most compelling Sauvignon Blancs — weighty, dry and minerally.

Price: **$28**

The vineyard, on the south bank of the Awatere River, is owned by Jean-Charles Van Hove, who has a winemaking degree from the University of Bordeaux, and his wife, Marguerite, both Belgians.

Since arriving in New Zealand in 1996, Jean-Charles has worked at Gladstone Vineyard, Corbans and Winegrowers of Ara. After buying their land in 1998, the couple chose to live on it, 'to observe the *terroir* and live the climate', before they planted their first vines in 2000.

Adjacent to Triplebank Vineyard, owned by Pernod Ricard NZ, Clos Marguerite lies on a gravel terrace, alongside a sheer, 14-metre drop to the river. The property has 8 hectares of vines (including 3 hectares of Pinot Noir) and an on-site winery, but no cellar door.

Clos Marguerite's vines are cultivated in

gravelly, free-draining soils overlying mudstone. 'For the viticulturist, this is heaven in terms of vine vigour,' says Jean-Charles, an expert on vineyard soils. The close-planted vines are low-yielding (only 7 to 10 tonnes of hand-picked grapes per hectare). The juice is cool-fermented in stainless steel tanks and the wine is lees-aged for several months before bottling.

What style of Sauvignon Blanc are they aiming for? 'It has a wonderful weight, texture and mouthfeel. The flavours are fresh and clean, carried by a fine acidity and delicate mineral character, yet offering a sumptuous array of ripe fruit characters.'

Clos Marguerite Sauvignon Blanc is a weighty, rounded wine, sweet-fruited and dry, that grows across the palate to a resounding finish. Much riper than most of the Awatere Valley's Sauvignon Blancs, it is powerful, concentrated and long.

'This is Marlborough Sauvignon Blanc, but not as you know it,' say the Van Hoves. 'It is for those who want an encounter, rather than just a drink.'

If you like this wine, also try: Tupari Marlborough Sauvignon Blanc; Tohu Marlborough Sauvignon Blanc

CLOUDY BAY
SAUVIGNON BLANC

>>> AFTER tasting the most famous Kiwi wine of all, writers tend to wax lyrical. Cloudy Bay Sauvignon Blanc has been praised as 'New Zealand's finest export since Sir Richard Hadlee' (David Thomas, *Punch*); 'Another gorgeous example of just how thrilling Sauvignon Blanc can be when it has such bright complexity — a riot of lime, guava and fresh celery notes…' (*Wine Spectator*); and as 'like hearing Glenn Gould playing the Goldberg variations, or seeing Niki Lauda at full tilt' (Mark Shields, *Sun Herald*, Melbourne).

Price: **$30**

An authoritative wine, Cloudy Bay Sauvignon Blanc is mouthfilling and finely scented, with beautifully ripe, zesty, melon/lime flavours that build to a crisp, dry, lasting finish. Weighty, complex and finely textured, it's a sophisticated — rather than pungently herbaceous — style, with great drinkability.

Launched from the 1985 vintage, the wine was an instant success. Wine lovers in the UK who wanted to buy the latest Cloudy Bay in the late 1980s joined a waiting list. Since then, production has skyrocketed and Cloudy Bay is now part of the Moet-Hennessy Louis Vuitton luxury goods group.

Chief winemaker Kevin Judd, who had been at the helm from the start, left at the end of the milestone 2009 vintage — the 25th for Cloudy Bay Sauvignon Blanc. The baton was passed to

Australian Tim Heath, who worked with Judd for five years, 'absorbing as much of his 25 years' worth of knowledge as I could'.

The grapes, grown in Cloudy Bay's own vineyards and those of long-term growers in the Wairau Valley, are mostly harvested by machine, with yields averaging 8 to 10 tonnes per hectare. The juice is mostly fermented in stainless steel tanks, but about 4 per cent of the blend is handled in old French oak barriques, 'to increase mouthfeel and palate weight'. Bottled in September, the wine is released by October, six months after the harvest.

Heath describes the 2010 as having 'characteristically uplifting aromas of ripe lime and grapefruit, nectarine, papaya and mango, and floral notes of orange blossom, gooseberry and sweet fennel. ... [The palate has] a chalky, weighty texture balanced by a minerally citrus acid backbone. The wine has elegant line and length: refined, fleshy yet focused and refreshing.'

Cloudy Bay Sauvignon Blanc is deliciously fresh and flavour-crammed in its youth, but it can also mature well for a decade, acquiring a food-friendly, toasty complexity. That the famous label has retained its impressive quality, while being built into sufficient volumes to be exported around the world, has been the greatest achievement of the Cloudy Bay team.

If you like this wine, also try: Clos Marguerite Marlborough Sauvignon Blanc; Clos Henri Marlborough Sauvignon Blanc

CLOUDY BAY TE KOKO

THIS intriguing, oak-aged Sauvignon Blanc is named after Te Koko o Kupe ('The oyster dredge of Kupe'), the original name for the bay on the Wairau Valley coast whose waters, when the river fills them with silt, turn cloudy.

A distinctive and unusually complex style of Marlborough Sauvignon Blanc, Te Koko is far from the regional norm. Rather than crisply herbaceous, it is deliciously sturdy, rich and rounded.

'Aromas of lemon thyme, mandarin blossom and stone-fruit combine harmoniously with ginger spice and nutty and savoury tones, underlined by exotic tropical notes,' is how Cloudy Bay described the 2007 vintage. 'The many-layered palate is creamy and textured.'

Price: $50

The origins of Te Koko lie in some lateral thinking in 1991 by newly recruited oenologist James Healy (now a partner in Dog Point Vineyard). Healy suggested to Kevin Judd, then chief winemaker, that it would be a good idea to ferment some Chardonnay with natural yeasts and give it a full, softening malolactic fermentation. Soon after, the talk turned to giving Sauvignon Blanc the same treatment.

Judd volunteered grapes from his own vineyard ('a gesture of support for wild things') and the result duly appeared at the cellar door as Cloudy Bay Sauvignon Greywacke Vineyard 1992. The first vintage of Cloudy Bay Te Koko finally arrived in 1996.

'Harvested in the cool of night, the grapes were gently pressed. The juice was settled for 48 hours and then racked into French oak barrels (10 per cent new) for its spontaneous and languid three-month primary fermentation. Eighteen months on yeast lees and a complete malolactic fermentation later, it was time to bottle the feral brew...'

Since Cloudy Bay's first experiments with an oak-aged Sauvignon Blanc, the style has been evolving constantly. The goal remains, however, of making a 'complete departure from Marlborough's internationally renowned, vibrant, zingy, fruit-driven Sauvignon Blanc style [in favour of] a limited edition creation that proudly challenges the safe and conventional.'

Flavour richness, ripeness and roundness are the hallmarks of Te Koko, coupled with complexity, a seductively creamy texture and enormous drinkability. Several other producers in the region have followed Cloudy Bay's lead and released barrel-aged Sauvignon Blancs, but none has surpassed Te Koko's quality.

If you like this wine, also try: Church Road Reserve Hawke's Bay Sauvignon Blanc; Dog Point Vineyard Section 94

COOPERS CREEK SV THE GROOVER GISBORNE GRÜNER VELTLINER

OUR cool climate for grapegrowing suits 'aromatic' white-wine varieties such as Riesling, Pinot Gris and Gewürztraminer. The latest arrival in the aromatic camp to stir up excitement here is Austria's signature white-wine grape, Grüner Veltliner.

Austrian wine is rare in New Zealand, but it is generally admired for its lightness, freshness and elegance. Grüner Veltliner covers over a third of Austria's total vineyard area, and is also established in the Slovak and Czech Republics, Hungary, the US, South America, China, Australia — and New Zealand.

Price: $21

Renowned for its versatility at the dinner table, Grüner Veltliner is described by Lettie Teague, a wine columnist for *The Wall Street Journal*, as having a 'spicy, peppery nose. The wines can be light and simple (a bright and refreshing aperitif), or rich and profound...'

Riversun Nursery, in Gisborne, six years ago imported two vineyard selections of Grüner Veltliner from Austria. Both have proved to be vigorous: 'Some management will be needed in the vineyard, as higher yields are known to produce inferior wines.' Coopers Creek, one of our most innovative producers of 'alternative' varieties, made New

Zealand's first Grüner Veltliner in 2008.

'There are thousands of different grape varieties and to concentrate on just a few of those is short-sighted,' Simon Nunns, winemaker at Coopers Creek, told the *New Zealand Herald*. 'New Zealand is a young winegrowing nation and we are still a long way from knowing what varieties will work here and what won't. The only way we will find out what works best is to keep experimenting.'

The 2010 vintage was hand-harvested from the Kawatiri Vineyard in Gisborne. After a cool fermentation in tanks, it was bottled in July with 13.5 per cent alcohol, moderate acidity and a barely perceptible touch of residual sugar.

Nunns is a senior wine judge, but admits he finds it 'hard to put a finger on descriptors' for the bouquet of his Grüner Veltliner. 'It has the white pepper character we expected, along with hints of ginger. This is backed by lees-derived aromas and a strong thread of flinty minerality.' He describes the palate as possessing 'lovely texture and mouthfeel. It is precise and focused, with a long, linear finish.'

The 2010 vintage of Coopers Creek SV (Select Vineyard) The Groover Gisborne Grüner Veltliner is the best to date. Floral and fleshy, it's a mouthfilling wine with dryish, peachy flavours, fresh and strong, hints of pineapples and spices, gentle acidity and a well-rounded finish. It's well worth discovering.

If you like this wine, also try: The Doctors' Marlborough Grüner Veltliner; Seifried Nelson Grüner Veltliner

CRAGGY RANGE LES BEAUX CAILLOUX

THIS is Craggy Range's flagship Chardonnay, a classy, weighty and concentrated wine, full of personality, with great mouthfeel, texture and depth.

The highest-profile winery to emerge in Hawke's Bay over the past decade or so, Craggy Range specialises in single-vineyard wines. 'For me, this is the ultimate winemaking challenge,' says Steve Smith, the company's wine and viticulture director. 'To work intensively in a vineyard, to understand it, and produce something with character that is entirely related to that special piece of land.'

Price: **$60**

Craggy Range's sweeping, 100-hectare Gimblett Gravels Vineyard is planted principally in Merlot, but also has significant areas of Cabernet Sauvignon, Syrah — and Chardonnay. 'Within the vineyard is an exclusive, very special parcel of Chardonnay that we have named Les Beaux Cailloux (the beautiful pebbles).'

In terms of style, the winemakers' goal is a 'complex, reserved, "bony" wine with hints of the intensity of New Zealand Chardonnay fruit, balanced with significant impact of winemaking. Power and lusciousness, balanced with a long, grainy finish.'

The grapes, very lightly cropped, are harvested by hand at an advanced ripeness level of 23 to 24 brix, and the juice is fermented with natural yeasts in French oak barriques (typically 45 to 70 per cent new). The wine has a full, softening malolactic fermentation and is bottled after a very lengthy period of barrel-aging — 14 to 17 months.

Robert Parker, the American wine guru, enthused about the 2002 vintage: 'It possesses a terrific texture yet great precision and elegance . . . there is no precedent for a Chardonnay such as this. . .'

Craggy Range describes the 2007 vintage as 'aromatically complex, with citrus blossom, lemon zest, peach and baguette crust. [It is] tightly woven, with taut acidity providing a tensile line through the palate which allows the complex flavours to unfold slowly. Summer fruits, cashew and faint vanilla spring to mind.' I see it as a majestic wine, notably refined, fragrant, weighty and deep. The 2008 is also powerful, complex, concentrated and creamy.

Craggy Range produces several other, lower-priced Chardonnays. The Gimblett Gravels Vineyard Chardonnay is a fully barrel-fermented wine, mouthfilling, citrusy and complex; the refined Kidnappers Vineyard Hawke's Bay Chardonnay, made using 'the traditional techniques of Chablis', is a subtle, gently oaked style, full of interest.

Wild Rock Pania Hawke's Bay Chardonnay (from a division of Craggy Range) is rich, sweet-fruited and creamy-textured, offering fine value at $20.

If you like this wine, also try: Church Road Tom Chardonnay; Craggy Range Gimblett Gravels Vineyard Chardonnay

DRY RIVER PINOT GRIS

DRY River has a cult following for its trickle of top-flight Martinborough wine. Its Pinot Noir, Gewürztraminer, Riesling and Chardonnay are all highly acclaimed — to say nothing of its impressive Viognier and Syrah — but in most wine lovers' eyes, the Dry River label is inextricably linked with Pinot Gris.

For many years after its debut in 1986, Dry River towered above other New Zealand Pinot Gris, by virtue of its exceptional body, flavour richness and longevity. 'There was a time when people only wanted to taste our Pinot Gris,' recalls the founder, Dr Neil McCallum. 'But the price [around $50] keeps it as a niche wine.'

Price: $50

What does Dry River Pinot Gris taste like? The first impression is of a satisfying sturdiness, from its high levels of alcohol and grape extract (stuffing). The flavours are deep, slightly sweet and rounded, with an array of stone-fruit, lychee and spice characters. Delicious in its youth, it can also flourish with cellaring.

Like the winery's equally lovely Gewürztraminer, the Pinot Gris is a rich Alsace style. The goal is 'concentrated, ripe flavours, with roundness and opulence when the wine is mature'.

Most of Dry River's Pinot Gris vines are over 30 years old. Sourced from Mission Vineyards, in Hawke's Bay, they are believed to be from a low-yielding Alsace clone, imported into New Zealand in 1886.

By holding the grapes on the vines until late April or early May, when they start to fall off, Dry River gives its customers a late-harvest wine in disguise. To avoid any loss of varietal flavours, it is not matured in oak, and it is bottled with 12 to 25 grams per litre of residual sugar, making it a medium-dry to medium style.

Since 2003, Dry River has been controlled by American businessman Julian Robertson, who also owns Te Awa winery in Hawke's Bay. However, McCallum is still involved as chief winemaker, with Katie Hammond as the 'hands-on' winemaker and her partner, Shayne Hammond, as Dry River's viticulturist.

At a vertical tasting in late 2009 of the 2004–2007 vintages, Dry River Pinot Gris 2007 stood out — gorgeously perfumed, with a rich, oily texture and striking depth of peachy, faintly honeyed flavour. At the tasting, next to me wine judge Bob Campbell murmured: 'That's the best Pinot Gris ever made in New Zealand.'

PINOT GRIS

2010

DRY RIVER

Martinborough

No. 2412

WINE OF NEW ZEALAND
D R WINES LTD, PURUATANGA RD, MARTINBOROUGH

If you like this wine, also try: Dry River Gewürztraminer Dry River Estate; Greystone Waipara Pinot Gris

ESK VALLEY HAWKE'S BAY VERDELHO

>>>

'SOME thing akin to a Riesling, with the body of a Chardonnay' is how Gordon Russell, winemaker at Esk Valley, describes New Zealand's best-known Verdelho (it's one of only three).

A Portuguese variety, long grown on the island of Madeira, Verdelho preserves its acidity well in warm grapegrowing regions. In Australia, for instance, it yields sturdy, citrusy, lively wines. Here, it's still extremely rare, with only 2 hectares of bearing vines recorded in 2011, mostly in Hawke's Bay.

Price: **$24**

Esk Valley's (and New Zealand's) first Verdelho flowed in 2002. Grown in the Gimblett Gravels, it had a distinct splash of sweetness, but in recent years has evolved into a dry to off-dry style.

Russell describes the 2010 vintage as 'a full-bodied, dry style, rich but with fresh acidity. Aromas and flavours of peach, musk and orange citrus predominate with a grapefruit-like acidity providing length.' I see it as a stylish, tightly structured and weighty wine with fresh, strong flavours of citrus and tropical fruits, and a mouth-wateringly crisp, dryish finish.

Esk Valley, which sourced its vines from Australia, planted its first block of Verdelho in 1998. 'The berries are small, the bunches loose, and it is one of the most delicious of all white grapes to eat,' says Russell. 'Our aim has been to translate this intensity into the bottle.'

The grapes are grown at two company-owned sites — the stony Omahu Gravels Vineyard, where the vines are now 13 years old, which provides the wine with 'a mineral-infused note and flavours of orange citrus'; and the Joseph Soler Vineyard, established in more fertile, silty gravels, which yields a 'richer, fuller wine style with flavours of tropical fruit'.

The grapes are hand-picked and about 60 per cent of the juice is fermented with natural yeasts in seasoned French oak casks, followed by a few months' aging on its yeast lees. About 40 per cent of the blend is cool-fermented in stainless steel tanks, 'to capture the pure, vineyard-derived aromatics and flavours'. The wine is bottled by August, its refreshing acidity balanced by a sliver of residual sugar.

Several years ago, Russell sent a case of the 2005 to a conference of Verdelho producers, staged in Western Australia. 'The wine caused quite a stir and some consternation as it was judged to be among the 12 best Verdelhos submitted and was therefore poured at the panel discussion and at the dinner afterwards.' Closer to home, the 2009 scored a gold medal at that year's Hawke's Bay A & P Mercedes-Benz Wine Awards.

So when should you drink this full-bodied and tangy white? Russell suggests serving it chilled, as 'the perfect match for all seafood'. It's also a stimulating partner for roast vegetables and creamy, coconutty Indian dishes.

If you like this wine, also try: Villa Maria Single Vineyard Ihumatao Auckland Verdelho; TW PT's Verdelho

FRAMINGHAM CLASSIC RIESLING

SAUVIGNON Blanc is the variety most Marlborough wineries trumpet to the world; Riesling is in the sales doldrums. But Framingham is a specialist in aromatic wines. 'Riesling is our flagship. ...'

Framingham Classic Riesling enjoys a strong international reputation. The 2008 vintage, for instance, won a blue-gold medal (judged with food) at the 2010 Sydney International Wine Competition, plus the trophy for best New Zealand Riesling at the 2009 *Decanter* World Wine Awards. In most years, it is a strikingly scented, flavour-packed and zesty wine.

Price: **$23**

Crafted in a medium style (typically harbouring 17 grams per litre of residual sugar), the Classic Riesling is based on low-cropped, leaf-plucked vines (which gives the fruit good exposure to sunlight). The grapes are picked mostly by machine: 'The short-term skin contact that occurs during machine-harvesting makes the wine more approachable early in its life.' The juice is tank-fermented at cool temperatures, stop-fermented with some natural sugar remaining, and matured for several months on its yeast lees 'to add texture'.

For winemaker Dr Andrew Hedley, Riesling is a personal favourite. Key attractions are the 'diversity of styles, its ageability and elegance'. His 2008 Classic Riesling, he says, possesses a 'lovely, fragrant, complex nose showing mandarin, honeysuckle, jasmine, green tea and lemon citrus aromatics, along with some wet stone-like minerality. ... Though tightly structured, the wine has a lovely, soft feel in the mouth.'

Raised in England, Hedley recalls his parents were 'not wine connoisseurs, but my father, a design engineer, used to visit Trier, on the Mosel, on business, and we would often open a bottle of wine at home on Sundays.' Later, while at university, Hedley visited southern Germany on a language course. 'A wine festival was on and we did lots of tasting. Little things like that intensify your interest, and then I started reading about wine.'

Not content with making one memorable Riesling, Hedley also produces a classic, slow-maturing Dry Riesling, limey and toasty; a partly barrel-fermented, medium-dry, F Series Old Vine Riesling, from vines planted in 1982; a *spätlese* style Select Riesling, late-picked, light and lovely; and a ravishing, honey-sweet Noble Riesling.

If you like this wine, also try: Pegasus Bay Riesling; Waimea Classic Riesling

NOV 2009

... equal portions of cabernet franc, pinotage, ... berryish, spicy flavours, showing considerable

... shelf price (eg in a su...

FROMM CLAYVIN VINEYARD CHARDONNAY

WHEN James Healy — a former oenologist for Cloudy Bay, who is now a partner in Dog Point Vineyard — once heard I was about to taste several years of Fromm Clayvin Vineyard Chardonnay, he looked envious: 'The 1996 vintage is the greatest Chardonnay ever produced in New Zealand.'

Tautly structured, bone-dry and minerally, rather than fresh and buoyantly fruity in the popular New World style, Fromm Clayvin Vineyard Chardonnay has a distinctly European feel. That's hardly surprising, when you consider the founders, Georg and Ruth Fromm, the current owners, Pol Lenzinger and Georg Walliser, and the winemaker, Hätsch Kalberer, are all Swiss.

Price: $56

The gently sloping, north-facing Clayvin Vineyard lies in the upper Brancott Valley. As its name suggests, most of the vineyard consists of various types of solid clay, which store moisture and reduce the need for irrigation. The clay soils exert a crucial influence on the personality of the wine. The Clayvin Vineyard Chardonnay is grown entirely in clay, while grapes from a relatively gravelly part of the vineyard are diverted to the lower-tier, unoaked, but still weighty and concentrated La Strada Marlborough Chardonnay.

Of the total vineyard area of 15 hectares, which also includes Pinot Noir and Syrah, only 1.5 hectares is earmarked for the Clayvin Vineyard Chardonnay.

The desired cropping level is only 5 tonnes of grapes per hectare, but even this is often not achieved, due to the low-yielding Mendoza clone's susceptibility to 'hen and chicken' (large and small berries).

Kalberer, who has guided Fromm's production since the first 1992 vintage, is looking for a 'scented, dry, minerally expression of the Clayvin Vineyard's *terroir* [soil, climate and topography], free from new wood flavourings. We appreciate a certain austerity in the wine's youth.'

In the winery, the grapes' natural balance and structure are preserved. The wine's acidity is never adjusted, it undergoes a full, softening malolactic fermentation, and is fermented to absolute dryness (even 1 to 2 grams per litre of residual sugar is not acceptable).

A total absence of new wood also contributes to the distinctive nature of Clayvin Vineyard Chardonnay. Only seasoned oak *pieces* (the traditional, 228-litre Burgundian equivalent of the 225-litre Bordeaux barrique) are used, ranging from two to six years old, due to the wine's long spell in wood (16 to 18 months) and, above all, Fromm's desire to express the site's *terroir*.

Fromm Clayvin Vineyard Chardonnay is a notably weighty, intense wine, powerful and generous, with a fine thread of acidity. With maturity it unfolds a strikingly complex bouquet: citrusy, mealy, minerally and nutty. Top vintages drink well for a decade.

If you like this wine, also try: La Strada Marlborough Chardonnay; Spy Valley Envoy Marlborough Chardonnay

GREENHOUGH HOPE VINEYARD PINOT BLANC

>>> GREENHOUGH, one of Nelson's best wine producers, started life as Ranzau, a tiny vineyard and winery established south-west of the city in 1979. When Ranzau's founder, Trevor Lewis, put a 1984 Müller-Thurgau/Pinot Blanc on the market, he must have raised a few eyebrows — every wine lover knew about Müller-Thurgau then, but Pinot Blanc was almost totally unknown.

It still is. A white mutation of Pinot Noir, Pinot Blanc is rated highly in Alsace, Germany, Italy and California for its fullness of body and gentle acidity. However, it is still rare in New Zealand, with only 17 hectares of vines bearing in 2011, mostly in Canterbury and Central Otago.

Price: $32

Andrew Greenhough and Jenny Wheeler, who purchased Ranzau in 1991 and changed its name to Greenhough in 1997, still have a few rows of Pinot Blanc vines planted by Lewis in 1979. The average age of their Pinot Blanc vines is 20 years.

Greenhough — who also produces outstanding Chardonnay, Sauvignon Blanc, Riesling and Pinot Noir — views Pinot Blanc as a versatile variety, equally suited to being made in a 'fruit-driven' or complex, oak-aged style. 'Either way, the wine has a rich, textural quality ... [and] like Gewürztraminer and Pinot Gris, it is naturally low in acidity.'

Top vintages of Greenhough Hope Vineyard

Pinot Blanc are full of interest — robust (with high alcohol, 14 to 14.5 per cent), weighty and rich, with concentrated peach, pear and spice flavours, slightly buttery and savoury. After some experimentation, Greenhough has settled on a barrel-fermented style that 'adds a gentle spice and complexity while allowing the fruit to remain in the foreground'.

The Pinot Blanc grapes are hand-picked from the Hope Vineyard, adjacent to the winery, where the vines are cultivated in deep river stones overlying sub-soils with a high clay content. The juice is fermented with natural and cultured yeasts in large, seasoned French oak casks and the wine is then barrel-aged, with regular stirring of its yeast lees, for a year.

The Wine Advocate, one of America's most influential wine publications, reviewed the 2009 Hope Vineyard Pinot Blanc in late 2010, praising its 'intense aromas of clover honey, apricots, poached pears and spiced apples. Dry, rich and full-bodied, it has a nice backbone of crisp acid cutting through silken texture and it gives a long finish. Superb wine with lots of character — I love it.'

So do I.

If you like this wine, also try: Gibbston Valley Central Otago Pinot Blanc; Greenhough Hope Vineyard Chardonnay

GREYSTONE WAIPARA PINOT GRIS

SINCE its first 'commercial' vintage in 2005, Greystone has stood out among Waipara's producers for a series of very classy aromatic white wines: Pinot Gris, Riesling and Gewürztraminer. Pinot Gris, the winery believes, is 'our most successful variety to date'.

It's benchmark stuff. Fragrant and full-bodied, it's a softly textured, medium style with stone-fruit, pear, lychee and spice flavours, showing lovely delicacy, ripeness, harmony and richness. The 2007 vintage won the trophy for top Pinot Gris in *Winestate*'s 2008 Wine of the Year Awards; the 2009 was the champion Pinot Gris of the 2009 New Zealand International Wine Show.

Price: **$29**

Bruce Thomas, whose family owns Greystone, is a former accountant. Dominic Maxwell, the winemaker, studied commerce before taking a postgraduate diploma in viticulture and oenology from Lincoln University. Since joining Greystone, Maxwell has worked at estates in Oregon (Chehalem), the Rheingau (Weingut Leitz) and Burgundy (Domaine D'Eugenie, in Vosne-Romanée.)

Viticulturist Nick Gill is an Australian. After working for Penfolds, managing the Magill Estate, Block 42, Koonunga Hill and Kalimna vineyards, in 2004 he shifted to New Zealand 'to work for people he could go fishing with'.

'When your grapes come from just one vineyard, there has to be a special understanding between the two people who are charged with growing the grapes and making the wine,' says Angela Clifford, Greystone's marketing manager (who is married to Gill). 'We jokingly refer to it as the "trans-Tasman bromance".'

The grapes are grown on the lower sections of the vineyard, in silty soils with limestone deposits, and harvested at a very advanced ripeness level of 24 to 25.5 brix. The juice is cool-fermented in stainless steel tanks and stop-fermented with residual sugar, creating a medium to medium-dry style. Lees-aging adds 'secondary flavours, such as brioche and bread'.

Greystone's latest move on the Pinot Gris front has been to launch an outstanding dry Pinot Gris, 'Sand Dollar', from the 2010 vintage. Harvested 'before the natural sugar levels got too high', it's a sturdy, deeply flavoured wine, peachy, spicy, tight and minerally, that carries the dry style perfectly.

If you like this wine, also try: Greystone Waipara Gewürztraminer; Greystone Sand Dollar Waipara Pinot Gris

HUNTER'S MARLBOROUGH RIESLING

HUNTER'S Marlborough Riesling topped *Cuisine*'s 2011 tasting of New Zealand Rieslings. That accolade was for the 2010 vintage. The 2009 also scooped a gold medal at the International Cool Climate Wine Show in Australia.

The name Hunter's is still linked, in most wine lovers' minds, to its classic Marlborough Sauvignon Blanc, first made in 1985, but the Riesling is no stranger to the show-judging circuit. The 1986 and 1989 were awarded gold medals at the Air New Zealand Wine Awards, and the 1993 and 1994 vintages won golds in a country that prides itself on Riesling — Australia.

Price: **$19**

Yet you can buy this consistently impressive, dryish wine for under $20. The style has evolved over the years, as a comparison of Hunter's 1988 'Rhine Riesling' with its 2008 Riesling makes clear. Both were picked with a similar level of sweetness (21 brix) in the grapes and fermented to an off-dry style (leaving 5 to 6 grams per litre of residual sugar). The major difference is that the 1988 vintage, with a total acidity of 9.2 grams per litre, was a far sharper, higher-acid wine than the 2008 (6.9 grams per litre).

'We used to make a very dry, austere Riesling

that would be good to drink in six or seven years, but it was all sold in six months,' winemaker Gary Duke told *Cuisine* recently. 'We've changed our approach. ... We now crop lower, have a dash more residual sugar and get riper flavours. The result is a wine that still has great acidic backbone and the ability to age well, but is more approachable in its youth.'

Duke aims for a full-bodied (around 13 per cent alcohol), dryish style with lively acidity. The grapes are machine-harvested in the early morning and the juice is cool-fermented in tanks with neutral yeasts. The winemaking is focused on retaining 'the maximum possible fruit aromas and flavours as seen in the vineyard'.

Scented, with rich, citrusy flavours and a long, finely poised finish, Hunter's Riesling is very fresh, lively and punchy. A stimulating apéritif and an excellent food wine, from one vintage to the next, it's a steal.

BEST BUY

If you like this wine, also try: Rippon Riesling; Valli Old Vine Central Otago Riesling

JACKSON ESTATE STICH MARLBOROUGH SAUVIGNON BLANC

⟫ 'STICH', in case you were wondering, is the nickname of John Stichbury, who founded the Jackson Estate label in 1991. Today, Stich and his team produce one of the region's most classy Sauvignon Blancs, weighty, dry and lingering, with lovely richness and roundness.

Stichbury's goal is a 'traditional Marlborough style of Sauvignon Blanc,

Price: **$22**

- - - - - - - - - - - - - - - - - - - -

meaning simple, direct, but clean and ripe fruit flavours. ... Achieving advanced fruit ripeness makes us successful.' In an early show triumph, the 1992 vintage won the trophy for champion Sauvignon Blanc at the 1993 International Wine Challenge.

Head winemaker Mike Paterson joined Jackson Estate in 2003, after experience in Burgundy, California's Sonoma Valley and the Hunter Valley in New South Wales. With Sauvignon Blanc, he says he aims for 'a dry food style, with a degree of restraint, that relies on fruit sweetness rather than residual sugar, and has good weight and texture rather than aromatic impact' — and hits the bull's-eye.

The grapes are drawn from several sites around the Wairau (mostly) and Awatere valleys, including the original Homestead Vineyard in Jacksons Road, in the heart of the Wairau Valley, where the unirrigated vines grow in heavy, moisture-retaining soils. Jackson Estate also owns vineyards at Rapaura and in the Omaka Valley, and buys fruit from contract growers.

For the 2009 vintage of Stich Sauvignon Blanc, 20 parcels of grapes were harvested over a four-week period (27 March to 24 April). Paterson, as winemaker, has no illusions of grandeur: 'Again, our heroes were found in our vineyards [run by Geoff Woollcombe]; supremely balanced vines, harvested at optimum ripeness, without compromise.'

The juice is fermented with cultured, neutral yeasts at low temperatures in stainless steel tanks. The young wines then spend several months on their light yeast lees before blending and bottling in early spring.

For a wine that is only slightly above average in price, Stich Marlborough Sauvignon Blanc is unexpectedly classy. Rich, vibrant and sweet-fruited, it has a lovely array of passionfruit, melon, lime and capsicum flavours, slightly minerally, crisp and long.

Jackson Estate also produces a single-vineyard Grey Ghost Sauvignon Blanc, fermented with natural yeasts and partly barrel-fermented. A more 'funky' style, it is very weighty and rich, with spicy, leesy, nutty notes adding complexity.

BEST BUY

If you like this wine, also try: Jackson Estate Grey Ghost Sauvignon Blanc; Palliser Estate Martinborough Sauvignon Blanc

JOHANNESHOF MARLBOROUGH GEWÜRZTRAMINER

JOHANNESHOF, a tiny winery alongside the highway from Picton to Blenheim, is the home of a gloriously perfumed, lush, flavour-packed Gewürztraminer. The 2010 vintage won gold medals and five-star ratings on both sides of the Tasman; in New Zealand alone, the 2009 scooped two trophies and four golds.

Price: **$31**

Deliciously soft and gently sweet, Johanneshof Gewürztraminer has lovely musky, exotic aromas, gentle acidity, and a powerful surge of ripe lychee and spice flavours. Business partners Warwick Foley and Edel Everling (born at Rudesheim, on the Rhine) produced their first wine together in 1991.

Foley believes Johanneshof Gewürztraminer compares well with those of Alsace — and he's right. After the 2003 vintage topped *Cuisine*'s annual Gewürztraminer tasting, I asked Edel how they achieved such a magical wine.

'There's a whole lot of reasons. Gewürztraminer is not easy to grow or make, because it's a delicate variety and you can easily lose the spiciness.'

The intense flavours 'start in the vineyard'. That year, the fruit was from first-crop vines at a contract grower's site in the lower Wairau Valley, picked over a week at a very ripe 23 to 25 brix.

In the winery, the partners aim for harmony: 'a balance of spiciness, sugar, acidity and alcohol'. Fermentation is with cultured yeasts in stainless steel tanks. Oak is not part of the recipe, but the wine is aged on its yeast lees.

In 2010, Johanneshof Marlborough Gewürztraminer 2004 became the first New Zealand wine to be inducted into the Octavian Vaults Library Collection in the UK. An extension of the International Wine Challenge, staged in London, the Octavian Collection is designed to demonstrate the cellaring potential of top wines.

At the Octavian Vaults tasting in 2009 of five-year-old wines, the Johanneshof 2004 was praised for its 'excellent Gewürztraminer aromatics. Spice, roses, pure. Sweet, juicy, ginger notes, really flavoursome, with great texture and freshness. Hedonistic, with a drinking window from now through to 2014.'

The same wine had earlier won the trophy for International Aromatic White Wine in the over £10 category at the 2005 *Decanter* World Wine Awards.

Gewürztraminer plays a key part in the Johanneshof selection. Foley and Everling also make a full-bodied, distinctly gingery Gewürztraminer Trocken/ Dry; a rich, slightly honeyed, sweet but not super-sweet Gewürztraminer Vendange Tardive; and even a grappa (grape-based brandy) based on Gewürztraminer.

If you like this wine, also try: Johanneshof Gewürztraminer Vendange Tardive; Lawson's Dry Hills Marlborough Gewürztraminer

KUMEU RIVER MATE'S VINEYARD CHARDONNAY

》》》 RARER and more expensive than its better-known, longer-established stablemate, Kumeu River Estate Chardonnay, Mate's Vineyard is the pinnacle of the West Auckland winery's Chardonnays. Winemaker Michael Brajkovich has likened Kumeu River Estate Chardonnay, a blend of grapes from several sites, to a 'village wine' and the single-vineyard Mate's Vineyard Chardonnay to 'a *premier cru* of the same village'.

Mate's Vineyard Chardonnay is similar to Kumeu River Estate Chardonnay,

Price: $55

- - - - - - - - - - - - - - - - - - - -

but slightly more opulent and concentrated. It offers the same rich and harmonious flavours of grapefruit, peach and butterscotch, but with even greater depth and with a stronger seasoning of new French oak in its youth.

For several years, the Brajkovich family had noted the characteristics of its various vineyard sites, and considered producing limited releases of single-vineyard wines to capture that individuality. Demand for the blended Kumeu River Estate Chardonnay prevented that move, until the launch of Mate's Vineyard Chardonnay from 1993 (followed in 2006 by two more single-vineyard Chardonnays, Coddington and Hunting Hill).

Mate's Vineyard lies straight across the road from the winery at Kumeu, on part of the original property purchased by the parents of the founder,

Mate Brajkovich, in 1944. Planting of the 2.5-hectare vineyard was completed in 1990. Mate Brajkovich died in 1992 — a year before the first harvest.

The 21-year-old vines are all of the low-yielding Mendoza clone. Only the finest grapes, from the lowest-vigour vines, are selected for the Mate's Vineyard label each year; the rest contribute to the multi-site Estate Chardonnay.

'When we harvested the first grapes from Mate's Vineyard in 1993, we knew the wine was going to be something very special,' recalls Michael Brajkovich. In the winery, the hand-picked grapes are handled similarly to the fruit for the Estate Chardonnay, with natural yeast fermentation and full barrel and malolactic fermentation. However, Mate's Vineyard sees slightly more new oak.

The Wine Spectator, in the US, praised the 2003 vintage (93 points) as 'taut, vibrant and complex, beautifully packed with classic Burgundian character. Has hazelnut, fig and green apple flavours at the core, weaving in nuances of lemon peel and mineral as the finish lingers.'

Powerful but not heavy, very refined, mealy and complex, top years of Mate's Vineyard Chardonnay are opulent, with concentrated, very ripe citrus and stone-fruit flavours, showing lovely richness and roundness.

If you like this wine, also try: Kumeu River Estate Chardonnay; Neudorf Moutere Chardonnay

LAWSON'S DRY HILLS MARLBOROUGH GEWÜRZTRAMINER

>>> ROSS Lawson could do anything, from mustering and shearing sheep to organising trade unions, hunting possums and building swimming pools. And he definitely knew how to make a great Gewürztraminer.

Right from the start — when most winemakers saw Gewürztraminer as an easy-drinking, slightly sweet wine with no prospect of greatness — the classic variety enjoyed a high profile in the Lawson's Dry Hills range. The 1992 vintage was an auspicious debut, with strong, spicy aromas, plenty of body and rich, citrusy, peppery flavours. A series of strikingly pungent wines followed, headily perfumed and overflowing with flavour. Today, this is one of New Zealand's most famous, consistently memorable Gewürztraminers.

Price: **$27**

Ross and Barbara Lawson planted their first vines in 1981, for a decade selling the crops to other companies. Ross, who died in 2009, attributed the Gewürztraminer's success to his vineyard sites and the clone.

'Both our home block, around the winery, and the Woodward Vineyard, down the road, have heavy clay soils, and we planted a great clone of Gewürztraminer. These two factors, combined with Marlborough's warmth in March, which ensures advanced ripeness

— while the cool nights retain the flavours — give extraordinary concentration in the grapes.'

The grapes, originally sourced from Penfolds (NZ), are now commonly identified as the 'Lawson's' clone of Gewürztraminer. The fruit is picked on flavour, typically at an advanced sugar level of 24 to 25 brix.

At the winery, on the eastern outskirts of Blenheim, near the sun-baked Wither Hills, the juice is mostly cool-fermented in stainless steel tanks, but a small component (about 7.5 per cent) is given 'the full treatment', with a high solids, natural yeast ferment in seasoned French oak barriques, malolactic fermentation and lees-stirring. The wine is bottled with a high average alcohol level of 14.5 per cent and 5 to 9 grams per litre of residual sugar, creating an off-dry style.

Exotically scented, it is lush and intensely varietal. A weighty wine with gentle acidity, it has highly concentrated lychee, spice and ginger flavours, very ripe and rounded. With cellaring, it deepens in colour, acquiring toasty, bottle-aged characters; top vintages mature well for up to seven years.

As a tribute to Ross, the winery has launched The Pioneer Marlborough Gewürztraminer. The debut 2009 vintage, harvested at over 25 brix, with some botrytis shrivel, and partly barrel-fermented, is powerful, with a voluminous bouquet and delicious intensity and softness.

If you like this wine, also try: Johanneshof Marlborough Gewürztraminer; Lawson's Dry Hills The Pioneer Marlborough Gewürztraminer

MILLTON CHENIN BLANC TE ARAI VINEYARD

>>>

FULL of personality and with a proven ability to flourish in the cellar for at least a decade, James Millton's Gisborne wine is the finest example of this country's most neglected white-wine variety — Chenin Blanc.

In 1986, Millton spent five weeks in France. 'The elusive Chenin Blanc variety attracted me to Vouvray ... [Here] the wines are a yardstick in terms of depth of flavour and aging ability, and its versatility is shown in the beautiful sweet wines from late-harvested fruit. There are many growers in this area of the Loire who grow their grapes along organic lines, and this was a bonus for me.'

Price: $30

In terms of style, Millton Chenin Blanc varies, depending on whether the growing season is hot or cool, dry or moist. 'But we want vinosity and texture, and a Chenin Blanc that will age. I want honey and acidity and almond flavours.'

In his pursuit of great Chenin Blanc, Millton sees soil and locality as of pivotal importance. 'Our Te Arai Vineyard at Manutuke is within five kilometres of the coast, so we get cooling sea breezes, which keeps up the acidity. Chenin Blanc needs that acidity for spine and longevity. And our soils are high in calcium, which Chenin Blanc likes.' Botrytis (noble rot) is generated by 'autumnal mists from the Te Arai Stream' which borders the vineyard on three sides.

The grapes are hand-picked over a month, culminating in the final harvest of botrytis-affected fruit. 'We pick some of the grapes when they're still green and malic, for their acidity. Then we pick ripe and fruity grapes, at around 20 to 23 brix, for texture. Finally — and it's in the lap of the gods — we pick for noble rot, which increases the wine's vinosity.'

Fermentation is mostly in large, 620-litre French oak casks called *demi-muids*, used in the Loire for Chenin Blanc. The yeasts are mostly natural, and over the winter, the wine is matured on its yeast lees, with occasional lees-stirring. It is bottled with moderate alcohol (typically 12 per cent) in an off-dry style (with around 10 grams per litre of residual sugar).

The 1987, 1988 and 1994 vintages all won the trophy for 'champion other white wine' at the Air New Zealand Wine Awards. Other top awards have followed, in Australia, the UK and the US, and James Millton notes that the wine 'continues to find favour in discerning markets'.

Millton Chenin Blanc Te Arai Vineyard is an intensely varietal wine. In dry seasons, it is tightly structured and buoyantly fruity, very fresh and crisp, with great aging potential. In wetter years, botrytis introduces a much more forward, honeyed character.

Both styles of Chenin Blanc reflect James Millton's lonely passion for the noble grape of Vouvray.

If you like this wine, also try: Esk Valley Hawke's Bay Chenin Blanc; Margrain Martinborough Chenin Blanc

MISSION JEWELSTONE HAWKE'S BAY CHARDONNAY

MISSION Vineyards occupies a unique place in New Zealand wine. By far the country's oldest winemaking enterprise, it is also our only nineteenth-century wine producer still under the same management. The jewel in the crown is its appropriately named Jewelstone Chardonnay.

Nestled at Greenmeadows, at the foot of the Taradale Hills near Napier, the vineyards and winery are run by the Catholic Society of Mary to fund its Marist seminary, which after 80 years at Taradale shifted to Auckland in 1990. In a peaceful setting of lawns and trees on an elevated site overlooking the winery, the former seminary building now serves as a restaurant and cellar-door operation. The Mission's wine sales still finance missionary work and the education of young men for the priesthood throughout New Zealand and the South Pacific.

Price: $34

For many years, the wines offered sound quality at a modest price, but today the Mission produces some excellent whites and reds. For winemaker Paul Mooney, who arrived at the Mission in 1979, Chardonnay is a special strength — from the standard, lightly oaked Hawke's Bay Chardonnay, flavoursome and creamy-smooth; to the sometimes top-value Vineyard Selection bottlings; fragrant, complex Reserve Chardonnay; and finally the powerful, robust Jewelstone Chardonnay, in top vintages a superbly concentrated, memorable wine.

The grapes for Jewelstone Chardonnay are grown in various districts of the Hawke's Bay region. The early releases during the 1990s were grown at Taradale. However, the 2001, 2002 and 2004 vintages were grown in Central Hawke's Bay; the 2006 and 2007 at Te Awanga, near the coast; and the 2008 in the Gimblett Gravels.

The grapes for the flagship Jewelstone label are hand-harvested from low-yielding vines (only 6 to 7 tonnes per hectare) and the juice is fermented in French oak barriques (40 to 50 per cent new). Natural yeasts and malolactic fermentation are key parts of the recipe, and the wine spends a long time in oak — about 17 months.

Top vintages of Jewelstone Chardonnay are powerful and tightly structured, with highly concentrated stone-fruit flavours, appetising acidity and lovely length. Mission is not a trendy label — it has been around far too long for that — but Jewelstone is well worth discovering.

If you like this wine, also try: Mission Reserve Hawke's Bay Chardonnay; Babich Irongate Chardonnay

MONTANA MARLBOROUGH SAUVIGNON BLANC

IF you take this world-famous wine for granted, fair enough. Seen on the shelves in every supermarket and corner store, it seems like it's been around forever. In fact, not until 1975 — two years after its initial flurry of plantings in Marlborough — did Montana take its spectacularly successful punt on Sauvignon Blanc. The first Montana Marlborough Sauvignon Blanc flowed in 1979.

Price: **$9–18**

Let's sort out two naming issues. Montana (owned by Pernod Ricard NZ) announced its name change to Brancott Estate in 2010. Only in New Zealand — and only on such low-priced wines as this — does the Montana label survive. Overseas, it is marketed as Brancott Estate Marlborough Sauvignon Blanc.

During the 1980s, Montana Marlborough Sauvignon Blanc created a stir, here and abroad. In choosing the 1986 vintage as 'Wine of the Year' in his 1987 *Good Wine Guide*, UK critic Robert Joseph declared that 'this remarkable New Zealand wine is not only a slap in the eye for all those producers of dull, over-priced Sancerre and Pouilly-Fumé, it is also one of the most deliciously and unashamedly fruity dry white wines I have ever tasted'.

The 1989 vintage won the Marquis de Goulaine Trophy for the champion Sauvignon Blanc at the

1990 International Wine and Spirit Competition in London. The 1991 vintage was crowned the champion white wine of the 1992 Sydney International Winemakers' Competition.

When the 1995 vintage was released, overseas buyers immediately ordered 46,000 cases. Today, the wine is still scooping top awards — the 2009 vintage won a gold medal at that year's Air New Zealand Wine Awards — and its annual production has soared to one million cases.

'Essentially, we have the right grape variety in the right place,' says Patrick Materman, chief winemaker for Pernod Ricard NZ. The grapes are grown mostly in the Wairau Valley, but since 2008 the inclusion of Awatere Valley fruit has added 'a more herbal note, vibrancy and aromatic lift'.

The machine-harvested grapes are generally crushed and their juice is left in contact with the skins for a few hours, 'to provide strength and fullness of flavour'; a smaller portion is gently bag-pressed, 'to achieve fresh, clear, elegant juice'. The wine is bottled young, in a basically dry style (3.5 to 4 grams per litre of residual sugar), with a moderate level of alcohol (12.5 per cent).

Aromatic, vibrantly fruity, flavourful and crisp, Montana Marlborough Sauvignon Blanc is a wine you can rely on, from one vintage to the next. When its price dips under $10, as it often does, it's an exceptional buy.

BEST BUY

If you like this wine, also try: Villa Maria Private Bin Marlborough Sauvignon Blanc; Saint Clair Marlborough Sauvignon Blanc

NEUDORF MOUTERE CHARDONNAY

>>> **THE** undisputed heavyweight of Nelson wines and arguably the greatest Chardonnay to flow from the South Island, Neudorf Moutere Chardonnay ranks among New Zealand's greatest wines of all. From their idyllic plot of vines in the blue-green hills of the Upper Moutere, Tim and Judy Finn produce a gloriously rich and multi-faceted Chardonnay that has often been compared to top white Burgundy.

Finn himself only partly accepts the comparison with Burgundy. 'Top Chardonnay from New Zealand is always fruitier than white Burgundy. I think it's because our sunlight is more intense. New Zealand's apples are very fruity. And we get higher levels of acidity in the grapes. But we *do* get some very similar flavour notes to white Burgundy in our wine,' says Finn.

Price: $55

Chardonnay has flowed from Neudorf's gentle clay slopes since 1982. In the region's typically long, warm summers with cool nights, Finn finds his Chardonnay gets 'very ripe, yet retains acidity. So we have the ability to ripen the grapes well, without any blowsiness. And the clay gives us deep, minerally, rather than effervescent, flavours. Our Chardonnay is largely prescribed by the *terroir* and the high-extract, high-acid Mendoza clone. The texture and complexity of long, barrel-stirred lees contact helps to balance this taut package.'

The vines, ranging up to 31 years old, are cultivated in sandy clay loam soils, threaded with layers of gravel, in the Neudorf Home Vineyard. The Mendoza clone is renowned for its 'hen and chicken' (large and small berries) effect, so at Neudorf the bunches are harvested when 'the large berries are ripe — the small berries are then very ripe'. Yields are low, generally under 7 tonnes of grapes per hectare.

The grapes are all picked by hand and their juice is run straight into barrels — French oak barriques and puncheons (30 to 40 per cent new). The primary, alcoholic fermentation is entirely with natural yeasts. All of the wine also goes through a softening malolactic fermentation, and is matured on its yeast lees in the barrels, with regular stirring, for a year.

Neudorf Moutere Chardonnay has great weight on the palate and exceptionally complex, citrusy, mealy, minerally flavours. That it is harder to track down than some other high-fliers — only 420 cases were produced of the 2009 vintage — is part of its appeal for those who have discovered this rare but brilliant gem.

If you like this wine, also try: Neudorf Nelson Chardonnay; Fromm Clayvin Vineyard Chardonnay

PALLISER ESTATE MARTINBOROUGH SAUVIGNON BLANC

THIS wholly seductive wine is one of the greatest Sauvignon Blancs in the country, with a distinguished track record in shows to prove it.

Yet Palliser Estate Sauvignon Blanc is distributed widely in New Zealand and overseas, proving it *is* possible to combine quality and quantity. It's a while ago now, but in three years out of four, the judges at the Air New Zealand Wine Awards gave the trophy for Best Commercial White Wine (minimum production of 1000 cases) to Palliser Estate Sauvignon Blanc (for the 2002, 2001 and 1999 vintages).

Price: $22

Grown in Martinborough, it is typically immaculate and overflowing with flavour. Ripe sweet-fruit aromas lead into a deliciously full-bodied wine with fresh, pure, incisive flavours of tropical fruits and capsicums and a crisp, sustained finish.

Winemaker Allan Johnson's goal is 'an intense style of Sauvignon Blanc, with flavours in the gooseberry/passionfruit spectrum. We want a rich, full and rounded wine with intense aromas, but it must be an easy-drinking style. People say that Sauvignon Blancs are acidic, but they often confuse acidity with a [hard] phenolic edge, which I go out of my way to avoid.' Great delicacy of flavour is one of the hallmarks of his wine. For Johnson, his Sauvignon Blanc is produced not in the winery but the vineyard. 'It's a combination of climate and viticultural techniques. In Martinborough we get day-long warmth, without cooling sea breezes, so the wine is slightly riper and richer than most of Marlborough's.' The timing of the harvest is crucial. 'We go through the vineyards about every three days, tasting the fruit, watching the flavours develop. You can select your wine style prior to the picking.'

Processing the grapes, harvested by machine, involves 'very careful winemaking,' says Johnson. 'We ferment the wine cool, with reasonably clear juice. There's no blending with Sémillon, no barrel fermentation, no oak-aging — the fruit gives us the breadth of flavour.' Basically a dry style, it is bottled with around 3 grams per litre of residual sugar.

A classy, distinctly cool-climate style of Sauvignon Blanc, despite its North Island origin, Palliser Estate offers an exquisite harmony of crisp acidity, mouthfilling body and fresh, incisive fruit flavours. It is widely recognised as the Martinborough district's leading Sauvignon Blanc.

Palliser Estate also makes a second-tier Sauvignon Blanc under the brand Pencarrow. Sometimes a blend of Martinborough and Marlborough grapes, it is low-priced and typically a great buy.

If you like this wine, also try: Pencarrow Sauvignon Blanc; Saint Clair Marlborough Sauvignon Blanc

PEGASUS BAY RIESLING

WHEN asked why Pegasus Bay Riesling is consistently outstanding, site is the first thing Ivan Donaldson, the company's founder, mentions. 'Waipara has long been recognised as a special Riesling area, ever since Corbans Private Bin [initially called Robard & Butler] Amberley Rieslings of the 1980s,' he says.

Pegasus Bay is North Canterbury's most acclaimed winery and Riesling is its most famous wine. At its best — and almost every vintage it's an exciting mouthful — Pegasus Bay Riesling is richly perfumed and strikingly intense, with searching flavours of citrus fruits, lime and honey, complex and luscious.

Price: $28

In Donaldson's view, Waipara's cold nights are a critical quality factor. 'Waipara has a similar amount of heat over the growing season as Marlborough, but night temperatures are lower, which extends the grapes' ripening period by about 10 days and enhances the development of terpenes [the flavour compounds associated with the floral aromas found in Riesling, Muscat and Gewürztraminer].'

Tucked up against the Teviotdale Hills, which provide shelter from cooling easterlies, the estate vineyard lies on terraces carved out of an old glacier bed by the Waipara River. The vines are cultivated in free-draining soils and the grapes are hand-picked, usually from the second week of May onwards.

In the winery, the juice is fermented long and cool, in stainless steel tanks, with a neutral strain of yeast. Once the desired balance of sweetness, acidity and alcohol has been reached (typically when the wine has 11 per cent alcohol and 25 to 30 grams per litre of residual sugar), the fermentation is arrested by chilling. The new wine is bottled with a high level of carbon dioxide, which can give it a slight *spritzig* tingle in its infancy.

A couple of years ago, nine of Germany's most prestigious producers — including Joh Jos Prüm, Dr Loosen, Egon Müller-Scharzof and Robert Weil — held a special Riesling tasting and dinner at the German Embassy in London. Six other wineries around the globe were invited to show what they could do with Riesling — including Pegasus Bay.

Pegasus Bay Riesling is a rich, distinctly medium style. The winery also produces a dry version, labelled Bel Canto; another scented, gently sweet Riesling under its lower-priced Main Divide brand; and two ravishing dessert wines, Pegasus Bay Aria Late Harvest Riesling and Pegasus Bay Encore Noble Riesling.

When the Donaldson family established their first vines at Waipara in the late 1980s, they were advised not to plant Riesling, on the grounds it wouldn't sell. 'Chris [Ivan's wife] insisted that we plant a block of Riesling, which we later extended, and now it's our biggest-selling wine.'

If you like this wine, also try: Main Divide Waipara Valley Riesling; Framingham Classic Marlborough Riesling

《《《

RIPPON RIESLING

A few winemakers could be wine writers if they chose, penning tasting notes about their own wines that are highly evocative. Nick Mills is winemaker at Rippon Vineyard, on the shores of Lake Wanaka. His parents, Rolfe and Lois, after several years of trial plantings, founded the district's first commercial vineyard in 1982.

Rippon Riesling is steely and minerally, in a distinctly cool-climate style with penetrating, lemony, appley flavours, a sliver of sweetness, firm acid spine and great longevity. Mills feels that Rippon Riesling makes anyone from Wanaka — the smallest and most northerly of Central Otago's sub-regions — feel right at home.

Price: $32

'Riesling, a clever child, picks up its soil character faster than any other variety,' he says. 'These vines ... produce a vinous expression of incredible accuracy. It is a wine of the land and speaks to me of home — Wanaka's crazy luminosity and its fruit of subdued elegance; the silica-based refractivity and flinty dryness of the soil; wildflower pollen blowing in the nor'-wester; the smell on the lake throughout the year.'

At 330 metres above sea level, the vineyard is one of New Zealand's highest. In a glacial moraine with free-draining schist soils, 15 hectares of vines have been planted, principally in Pinot Noir and Riesling.

From mature vines, planted between 1987 and

1991, the Riesling grapes are harvested by hand and the juice is fermented with natural yeasts in a large, horizontal, stainless steel tank. After a couple of months on its yeast lees, it is bottled with a high level of total acidity (9 grams per litre in 2008) and a gentle splash of sweetness. Each vintage is matured for a year prior to its release.

It ages well. More than a decade ago, Central Otago winemakers gathered at Rippon for barrel tastings of the region's Pinot Noirs from 1999 and a vertical tasting of every vintage of Rippon Riesling from 1991 to 1999. One of the winemakers' favourites was the 1991, then eight years old, described as 'classic German-style Riesling. Secondary [bottle-aged] flavours coming through, with a good mid-palate weight. Fresh lime flavours give this wine the ability to age much, much longer.'

Top vintages of Rippon Riesling are Mosel-like, with great intensity, a strong presence and a resounding finish.

Mills also produces a Jeunesse Young Vines Riesling, from vines planted in 2000. 'Not yet old enough to recount the complexity of their soils, vines in their youth (or *jeunesse*) produce fruit that remains a pure and precise expression of their variety,' he says. Tight, vibrant and minerally, it's delicious in its youth.

If you like this wine, also try: Rippon Jeunesse Young Vines Riesling; Valli Old Vine Central Otago Riesling

SACRED HILL RIFLEMANS CHARDONNAY

≫ 'POWER and elegance' are winemaker and part-owner Tony Bish's key goals for Sacred Hill's flagship Hawke's Bay Chardonnay. 'We're really passionate about the wine,' he says. 'When we blind-taste our way through all the barrels, selecting for the Riflemans label, we spend days on the job. We're not pursuing a blockbuster style. The power comes on the finish, rather than upfront — Riflemans has to be classy.'

Price: $54

Bish, who in the mid-1980s was the company's vineyard manager, describes himself as 'very much a "vineyard winemaker", putting into practice the adage that the best wines are made in the vineyard'.

On a spectacular site overlooking the Tutaekuri River, the Riflemans Terrace Vineyard is planted wholly in Chardonnay. The vineyard lies at the head of the Dartmoor Valley, 20 kilometres inland and 100 to 115 metres above sea level, on the edge of sheer limestone cliffs.

The inland, elevated location of the Riflemans Terrace Vineyard has a powerful influence on the wine's quality and style. 'It's cooler than down on the plains, and you get greater length of flavour. Even at 24 brix [a high sugar level], the grapes hold their natural acidity.'

The Mendoza-clone vines for Riflemans Chardonnay were planted 22 years ago in free-draining red metal soils of very low fertility. The grapes are hand-harvested with an ultra-low average yield of only 3 to 4 tonnes per hectare.

Sent straight to barrel with high solids in the juice, Riflemans Chardonnay is fermented with natural yeasts in French oak barriques (new and one-year-old), and malolactic fermentation varies from 25 per cent to 100 per cent. The wine stays on its yeast lees for its whole life in barrel, which is usually 12 months, with regular lees-stirring.

Sacred Hill produces numerous Chardonnays, including those under its Whitecliff, Gunn Estate and Wild South brands. The Sacred Hill range includes a peachy, vibrantly fruity Hawke's Bay Chardonnay; a barrel-fermented Halo Hawke's Bay Chardonnay, citrusy and crisp; and a full-bodied, peachy and toasty, well-rounded The Wine Thief Series Chardonnay, made in the classic regional style.

Bish describes the much-awarded Riflemans Chardonnay as having 'a peachy mid-palate and the flavour of lemon meringue pie on the finish'. An outstanding wine with power, elegance, intensity and harmony, it is sturdy, rich and refined, with a strong surge of citrusy, mealy, minerally flavours, threaded with fresh acidity, and a lasting finish.

If you like this wine, also try: Sacred Hill The Wine Thief Series Hawke's Bay Chardonnay; Babich Irongate Chardonnay

SAINT CLAIR MARLBOROUGH SAUVIGNON BLANC

NEAL and Judy Ibbotson planted their first vines in 1978. Of the throng of grape-growers turned winemakers in the region, the Ibbotsons — who now run the largest family-owned winery in Marlborough — have achieved the most eye-catching success.

The debut 1994 vintage of Saint Clair Marlborough Sauvignon Blanc won a gold medal, and since then the flow of awards has been exceptional.

Price: $21

The 2005 vintage won six gold medals and three trophies in New Zealand and Australia; the 2010 won a gold medal at the 2011 Royal Easter Show Wine Awards.

Ibbotson concedes he's no winemaking expert — his strength is getting the best out of his vineyards and growers. Saint Clair's positioning statement, 'A Growing Reputation', shows the importance it places on viticulture.

For Sauvignon Blanc, its preferred sites are mostly in the lower reaches of the Wairau Valley. 'The soils are all fertile, free-draining and even; the climate is cool; the hang-time [of the grapes on the vines] is generally long. There is uniformity in vine growth, crop level and ripening; there is good light exposure; no disease; no nutrient or moisture stress; and the management is exceptional.' His key focus, says Ibbotson, is 'ensuring that we pick our grapes when they are at their optimum flavour profile'.

At the winery, the grapes, harvested by machine, are pressed immediately to minimise skin contact. The juice is settled, then cool-fermented with cultured yeasts in stainless steel tanks, 'to retain fruit flavour and freshness'.

All the batches of Sauvignon Blanc are kept separate and, before blending, are scored by a winemakers' tasting panel. Of Saint Clair's total production of Sauvignon Blanc, the top 3 per cent is earmarked for its small-volume Wairau Reserve and Pioneer Block bottlings, but the next 30 per cent is earmarked for this wine. (The rest is sold under Saint Clair's cheaper Vicar's Choice label, or marketed under other brands.)

Saint Clair describes the 2010 vintage as 'a full, crisp and powerful wine showing intense flavours of passionfruit and blackcurrant, with underlying gooseberry tones. This wine has a full yet elegant palate with subtle minerality. Well balanced acidity gives a long, lingering finish.'

For such a large-volume label, sold in more than 50 countries, Saint Clair Marlborough Sauvignon Blanc is remarkably good and fully a match for many producers' reserve bottlings. It's sharply priced, too.

BEST BUY

If you like this wine, also try: Saint Clair Wairau Reserve Marlborough Sauvignon Blanc; Jackson Estate Stich Marlborough Sauvignon Blanc

SEIFRIED WINEMAKER'S COLLECTION NELSON GEWÜRZTRAMINER

SEIFRIED is the largest winery in Nelson, with a reputation for good, often excellent, wines at affordable prices. For decades, it has championed Riesling and Gewürztraminer, both 'aromatic' varieties cultivated in Hermann Seifried's homeland, Austria. My favourite is this hedonistic, exotically perfumed beauty.

Price: **$23**

Full of personality, it is an oily-textured, typically medium-dry style (although sometimes a bit sweeter), with peach, apricot, lychee, ginger and spice flavours, deliciously rich, ripe and rounded. Softly mouthfilling, it has pure, intense flavours, showing lovely delicacy and harmony, and its soaring, musky aromas are instantly inviting.

Hermann Seifried takes pride in his long-term crusade for Gewürztraminer. 'We stuck with Gewürztraminer when everyone else was pulling it out [during the government-funded vine-pull scheme of 1986]. Now every year we sell thousands of cases.'

The grapes were originally from Seifried's oldest Gewürztraminer vines, in the Redwood Valley, at the foot of the Moutere hills. However, since the 2009 vintage, they have been grown in stony, infertile soils in the company's sweeping vineyard at Brightwater, 15 kilometres inland on the Waimea Plains, where irrigation water is drawn from a huge dam built by Seifried.

Gewürztraminer is an early-ripening variety, allowing the grapes to be harvested by mid to late March. After a brief period of skin contact — to boost flavour — the juice is cool-fermented in stainless steel tanks. To retain slight sweetness, the fermentation is stopped prematurely, and the wine is blended and bottled by July, allowing 'the fruit to really take front stage'.

Seifried Winemaker's Collection Nelson Gewürztraminer performs strongly on the show circuit. The 2009 vintage was rated 4.5 stars by *Winestate* magazine; the 2010 won a gold medal and the trophy for champion Gewürztraminer at that year's Romeo Bragato Wine Awards.

If you love 'Gewürz', also try Seifried Nelson Gewürztraminer, a well-spiced, flavourful wine which can rival its slightly higher-priced stablemate for floral, musky charm. The 2010 vintage also yielded a very good, bargain-priced Gewürztraminer under the company's Old Coach Road brand.

BEST BUY

If you like this wine, also try: Seifried Nelson Gewürztraminer; Lawson's Dry Hills Marlborough Gewürztraminer ❮❮❮

SELAKS WINEMAKER'S FAVOURITE HAWKE'S BAY CHARDONNAY

>>>

SELAKS in 2009 celebrated the 75th anniversary of its 1934 vintage debut, produced at Te Atatu, in West Auckland, by Croatian immigrant Marino Selak. Today, Selaks is one of the major brands of this country's second-largest wine producer, Constellation New Zealand (formerly Nobilo Wine Group).

Richly flavoured and smooth, this affordable wine is consistently a great buy.

Price: **$21**

Generous, with ripe, stone-fruit flavours seasoned with toasty oak, it is creamy-textured, with good harmony — and great drinkability.

When Nobilo purchased Selaks 13 years ago, it acquired another long-established Kumeu wine company. It also picked up Selaks' extensive vineyards and a gleaming winery in Marlborough, and Selaks' brands (better entrenched than Nobilo's in the premium wine market).

Brett Fullerton, Selaks' head winemaker, gained a postgraduate diploma in oenology (winemaking), but still considers himself to be 'a tradesman of wine, rather than a scientist'. Barrel-fermented Chardonnay is one of his favourite styles.

Launched in 2006, with wines from current and older vintages, the Winemaker's Favourite range stood out immediately for its combination of excellent quality and moderate prices, and has collected a swag of awards. The debut 2005 vintage, labelled 'Selaks The Favourite Hawke's Bay Chardonnay', was excellent, and since then the wine hasn't looked back. *Winestate* praised the 2006 as 'weighty, concentrated and complex, with ripe tropical-fruit flavours, creamy, nutty, buttery notes, and lovely depth, texture and harmony. A great buy.'

Since the 2008 vintage, which won two gold medals and a trophy, the wine has been labelled Selaks Winemaker's Favourite Hawke's Bay Chardonnay. The grapes have generally been grown in the sweeping, company-owned Corner 50 Vineyard in Hawke's Bay, but the 2009 vintage was drawn from sites closer to the coast, at Bay View and Haumoana.

Fermented, mostly with natural yeasts, in new and seasoned French oak barriques, the wine is matured for about eight months on its yeast lees and a significant proportion of the blend has a softening malolactic fermentation (50 per cent in 2008, 85 per cent in 2009).

The Selaks Winemaker's Favourite line-up also includes a bargain-priced Hawke's Bay Pinot Gris, Syrah and (especially recommended) Merlot/ Cabernet; a 'full-on' Marlborough Sauvignon Blanc, and a floral, supple Central Otago Pinot Noir. But don't miss the Chardonnay, unexpectedly powerful, rich, complex and creamy for its price.

BEST BUY

SELAKS
WINEMAKER'S FAVOURITE
HAWKE'S BAY
CHARDONNAY
13.5%Vol | NEW ZEALAND WINE

If you like this wine, also try: Church Road Hawke's Bay Chardonnay; Mission Jewelstone Hawke's Bay Chardonnay

⟪⟪

SERESIN MARLBOROUGH SAUVIGNON BLANC

THIS is a noteworthy wine, for three reasons — one of the country's greatest Sauvignon Blancs, it is marketed around the world and has full organic certification from BioGro.

Right from the start in 1996, Michael Seresin, a New Zealand-born film-maker based in the UK, and his winemaker, Brian Bicknell (who left in 2006) chose to move away from the prevailing 'fresh and fruity' style of Sauvignon Blanc and aim for a wine that was 'more subtle on the nose, offering some textural interest on the palate and had some complexity too'.

Price: $27

Seresin Estate's vineyards have always been run on organic and biodynamic principles. 'I just believe it's right,' says Michael Seresin. 'In essence it's traditional agriculture, it's how it was done before the chemical age came along, and wine's been around a lot longer than the chemicals have.'

The grapes are hand-harvested from three company-owned sites. Most are grown in the original vineyard west of Renwick, where the vines are planted on the cooler and higher of two terraces, in a mix of silt, stones and clay. Further grapes are drawn from the Tatou Vineyard, further inland, where the vines are planted in very stony soils and give a more aromatic, leaner style of Sauvignon Blanc; and the elevated, north-facing Raupo Creek Vineyard in the Omaka Valley, planted in clay-rich soils.

Sémillon — typically 5 per cent of the final blend

— is added for its distinctive 'nettley' character and to enhance the wine's flavour length. At the winery, the grapes are sorted on a 'triage' table, and the batches from the many blocks are fermented separately, to give more options when creating the final blend. To enhance the wine's complexity and texture, it is fermented with natural (mostly) and cultured yeasts, predominantly in tanks, but about 15 per cent of the blend is fermented in aged French oak barriques. Regular *batonnage* (lees-stirring) adds yeasty, creamy notes.

Winemaker Clive Dougall describes the 2009 vintage as 'finely textured with gooseberry, zesty citrus and mineral flavours combined with a slight creaminess. A firm acidity helps to draw out the finish.'

A sophisticated wine, Seresin Marlborough Sauvignon Blanc is full of individuality and interest. One of the region's most subtle and satisfying Sauvignon Blancs, it is rich and complex, but the barrel fermentation and lees-aging do not overwhelm its pure, penetrating fruit flavours.

Seresin also produces three other Sauvignon Blancs: a fully barrel-fermented Marama Sauvignon Blanc, sturdy, concentrated, sweet-fruited and nutty; a very ripely scented, passionfruit, pear and spice-flavoured Reserve Sauvignon Blanc, handled in tanks and seasoned casks; and a full-bodied, dry, tropical fruit-flavoured wine under its lower-priced Momo brand.

CERTIFIED ORGANIC

SAUVIGNON BLANC
MARLBOROUGH
NEW ZEALAND

If you like this wine, also try: Seresin Marama Sauvignon Blanc; Clos Henri Marlborough Sauvignon Blanc

《《《

SPY VALLEY ENVOY MARLBOROUGH CHARDONNAY

NAMED after a pair of huge white spheres, used for monitoring satellite communications, in the Waihopai Valley, Spy Valley is regarded highly by many wine lovers for its full-bloomed, richly flavoured aromatic whites, Riesling, Gewürztraminer and Pinot Gris. But don't miss this tight, elegant and minerally Chardonnay, a Burgundian style with great intensity, finesse and personality.

Price: **$40**

The vines are grown on a sheltered, lower terrace in the company's 150-hectare Johnson Estate Vineyard, planted since 1993. 'The fruit for Envoy is taken from a unique corner of one of our original Chardonnay blocks,' says Spy Valley. 'Block B' is home to five Burgundian clones of Chardonnay. 'The soil structure gives the best of both worlds — structure and fatness from the more complex topsoil, and fruit definition from the free-draining nature of the underlying gravel.'

Chief winemaker Paul Bourgeois, a third-generation Kiwi with French ancestry, has the grapes picked by hand when fully ripe (around 23 brix) and the juice is barrel-fermented with natural yeasts. The wine all goes through a softening malolactic fermentation and is matured in barrels, on its full yeast lees, for 18 months.

If you like your Chardonnay big and buxom, Envoy is not for you. The goal is a wine that is 'tightly structured around a core of exceptional fruit, pure, fine and long'. Bourgeois wants 'a precise and focused palate with a cleansing, mineral finish. Delicate hazelnut and complex secondary flavours will emerge with bottle age.' Finesse and longevity, rather than bold, upfront appeal, define Envoy.

Spy Valley also produces a popular Unoaked Marlborough Chardonnay, fleshy, fresh and full-flavoured, with drink-young appeal and a very smooth finish. The middle-tier Spy Valley Marlborough Chardonnay, hand-picked and mostly barrel-fermented, is always attractive, with finely balanced, citrusy, peachy flavours, showing some savoury complexity.

Top vintages of Envoy rank among Marlborough's most refined Chardonnays. Fragrant and full-bodied, with citrusy, complex, slightly creamy flavours, a fine thread of acidity and a long finish, it's a wine of true distinction.

If you like this wine, also try: Spy Valley Marlborough Chardonnay; Fromm Clayvin Vineyard Chardonnay

STONELEIGH MARLBOROUGH CHARDONNAY

IT'S easy to underestimate the quality of this long-popular wine. Its suggested retail price is over $20, but in supermarkets, where it is mostly sold, the average sale price is under $15.

Yet wine judges keep giving it top accolades. The 2009 vintage scooped a gold medal at the New Zealand International Wine Show 2010, and the 2008 won gold at the New World Wine Awards 2009. It's no surprise, really. The 2003 vintage topped Cuisine magazine's tasting of sub-$20 New Zealand wines, and the 1996 vintage won a White Wine of the Year trophy at the International Wine Challenge, in London, in 1998.

Price: $15-22

Made by the country's largest producer, Pernod Ricard NZ, this wine is always enjoyable, in a smooth, slightly creamy style with very good texture and richness — and plenty of drink-young appeal.

The Stoneleigh selection, which also includes Sauvignon Blanc, Riesling, Pinot Gris and Pinot Noir, is grown in the Rapaura district, on the gravelly, northern side of the Wairau Valley. According to Pernod Ricard NZ: 'The unique, stony, free-draining alluvial soils, together with the slightly warmer climatic conditions of the Rapaura area, produce fruit that ripens earlier than other regions of Marlborough.'

The grapes are harvested by machine at a ripe 22 to 24 brix, and the juice is fermented and lees-aged in a mix of French oak barrels (typically 60 per cent) and stainless steel tanks (40 per cent). About half the blend undergoes a softening malolactic fermentation, and it is bottled with a virtually imperceptible sliver of sweetness (4.7 grams per litre of residual sugar in 2008; 5.1 grams per litre of residual sugar in 2009).

Jamie Marfell, Stoneleigh's winemaker, grew up on a Marlborough farm that overlooked vineyards. He views the wine as 'a rich, ripe style with layers of complexity from careful oak management and lees-stirring while maturing in oak'. With its stone-fruit flavours and barrel-ferment complexity, Marfell argues fairly that Stoneleigh Chardonnay has a tradition of 'punching above its weight'.

Also well worth trying is Stoneleigh Rapaura Series Marlborough Chardonnay, slightly higher-priced. Fermented and lees-aged for four months in French oak barriques (much longer in earlier vintages), it's a 'fruit forward' style, but still complex — generous, creamy, nutty and long.

BEST BUY

If you like this wine, also try: Stoneleigh Rapaura Series Marl-borough Chardonnay; Selaks Winemaker's Favourite Hawke's Bay Chardonnay

TERRACE EDGE WAIPARA VALLEY PINOT GRIS

FROM one vintage to the next, this opulent, hard-to-resist wine offers wonderful value. Richer and more complex than most New Zealand Pinot Gris, it is enticingly scented, with substantial body, a hint of honey, gentle sweetness and deliciously rich peach, nectarine and spice flavours.

Terrace Edge is a small vineyard and olive grove on the south bank of the Waipara River, in North Canterbury. Since purchasing the land — formerly used for grazing sheep — in 1999, Bruce and Jill Chapman and their family have planted 12 hectares of Pinot Gris, Riesling, Pinot Noir and Syrah vines. (They also have an olive grove with 2000 trees, producing gold medal-winning olive oil.)

Price: $21

The vineyard, run by Peter Chapman — Bruce's and Jill's youngest son — is cultivated in silt loam soils of relatively low fertility, which reduces the plants' vigour and produces small crops (in 2010, just 5 tonnes per hectare). The grapes are all estate-grown and hand-picked.

Terrace Edge's first wines flowed in 2005. They are made by Belinda Gould, a former viticulturist who was, until recently, best known as the winemaker for one of Waipara's top producers, Muddy Water. After gaining a diploma in horticulture at Lincoln University in 1979, she spent two years studying viticulture at the famous

Geisenheim Institute in the Rheingau. After working as a research technician, Belinda joined Waipara Springs as assistant winemaker in 1993, and later held senior winemaking positions in California, at the Calera and Sonoma-Cutrer wineries.

For its Pinot Gris, Terrace Edge's goal is 'a rich, aromatic wine with good complexity. . . Varietal flavours are accumulated through hangtime on the vines well into autumn [from late April to early–mid May]. Fermentation is with native yeasts in aged oak barriques and the lees is stirred.'

Cropping the vines lightly; hand-picking late-harvested grapes (typically at a super-ripe 25 brix); barrel fermentation with natural yeasts; aging the young wine on its yeast lees; stirring the lees several times daily for a month; these are all crucial parts of the recipe for this memorable wine.

Praised widely by critics and retailers, and a gold medal winner (the 2009 at the Royal Easter Show Wine Awards 2010), Terrace Edge Waipara Valley Pinot Gris is a consistently impressive wine, full of flavour and personality.

Why they sell it for just over $20 is a mystery. It's as good as some Pinot Gris asking twice that price.

If you like this wine, also try: Terrace Edge Waipara Valley Riesling; Greystone Waipara Pinot Gris

TE WHAU VINEYARD WAIHEKE ISLAND CHARDONNAY

Te Whau Vineyard — named after a small coastal tree — climbs a steep, north-facing slope on Waiheke Island, topped by a classy, much-awarded restaurant offering glorious views across the harbour to Auckland. Its signature red, The Point, is a very classy, distinctly Bordeaux-like blend, but the rare, ravishingly beautiful Chardonnay is arguably its greatest wine.

Price: $85

Te Whau Vineyard Chardonnay is powerful and full of personality, with substantial body and highly concentrated, ripe stone-fruit flavours, rich, nutty and creamy-smooth. 'Jamie Oliver, a.k.a. The Naked Chef, took a case back to London in his hand luggage following his visit to our restaurant last summer,' reported the Te Whau newsletter for autumn 2002.

Tony Forsyth, a psychologist, formerly headed the personnel consultancy firm Sheffield. 'This is my second career,' he says. The tiny vineyard is protected from cool southerly winds, and the three-level winery under the restaurant uses gravity, rather than pumps, to move the grape juice and wine. Swiss winemaker Herb Friedli joined Te Whau before the first 1999 vintage.

'Our Chardonnay site is incredibly sheltered

and warm,' says Forsyth. But of Te Whau's total plantings of 2.3 hectares, only 0.3 hectares are devoted to Chardonnay.

In most years, the production amounts to just four barrels of wine. The 2008 vintage — the tenth — was hand-picked and fermented with natural yeasts in a mix of new, one and two-year-old French oak casks, where it matured for a year, with lees-stirring.

Forsyth and Friedli aim for a wine of 'elegance and subtlety'. It's also an exceptionally concentrated Chardonnay, with sweet, ripe-fruit characters seasoned with biscuity oak, notable complexity and a long, finely poised finish.

Te Whau recently opened every vintage of its Chardonnay from 1999 to 2008. The 1999 still offers pleasure and the tight, elegant 2001 is now at its peak. Others (2000, 2002) were a bit past their best, but the delicious procession of 2003 to 2006 vintages showed the wines' ability to flourish for at least five to seven years.

Kitty Johnson, daughter of the great English wine writer Hugh Johnson, praised the 2003 vintage for its 'wonderfully rich spiced-pear nose, luscious palate of honey and peach and long, crisp finish'. Johnson himself has compared Te Whau Chardonnay to the *grand cru* Corton-Charlemagne (from Burgundy), describing it as 'intense . . . finely structured . . . truly sumptuous'.

If you like this wine, also try: Craggy Range Les Beaux Cailloux; Kumeu River Mate's Vineyard Chardonnay

THE DOCTORS' MARLBOROUGH ARNEIS

FOR a wine lover looking for exciting new experiences, Italian wine is an obvious choice, smelling and tasting intriguingly different.

New Zealand's pioneer winemakers simply planted the grape varieties they were familiar with. Classic French and German varieties — Sauvignon Blanc, Chardonnay, Riesling, Pinot Gris, Pinot Noir, Merlot, Cabernet Sauvignon, Syrah — are the source of the majority of our wine. But a rivulet of wine from traditional Italian grapes signals an intriguing new direction.

Price: $25

Arneis (pronounced 'Are-nay-iss') is still so rare here it is not listed separately in the latest national vineyard survey. A traditional grape of Piedmont, in north-west Italy, where it yields soft, early-maturing white wine with slightly herbaceous aromas and almond flavours, Arneis was first planted in New Zealand in the late 1990s at Clevedon Hills vineyard in South Auckland. Coopers Creek released the country's first varietal Arneis in 2006.

Under its separate brand, The Doctors', Forrest Estate produces a deliciously floral and fleshy Arneis with a basket of flavours — peach, pear, apple and spice — and a dryish, rounded finish. Dr John Forrest (who has a doctorate in biomedical sciences) and his wife and business partner, Dr Brigid Forrest (a GP), say The Doctors' label is all about innovation: 'New grape varieties, alternative winemaking techniques and select parcels of fruit...'

The Forrests planted Arneis in a stony part of their Gibson's Creek Vineyard, in the heart of the Wairau Valley, hoping the 'classic, free-draining silty/stony *terroir*' will give the wine 'its signature wet-stone minerality'. The word Arneis means 'little rascal', which Forrest Estate says reflects its tricky character in the vineyard. A vigorous variety, it needs careful tending.

The grapes are hand-harvested from low-yielding vines (5 to 7 tonnes per hectare) and the juice is cool-fermented in stainless steel tanks. The wine is bottled young, with an alcohol level of around 13.5 per cent, refreshing acidity, and a whisker of sweetness.

John Forrest views Arneis as 'a different and alluring wine' that shows real potential in Marlborough's cool climate. His Arneis 'abounds on the nose with pears, white flower, fennel and fresh herbs — sage and rosemary. The palate shows stone-fruit and dried herb notes, textured, minerally, and with that classic Arneis dry finish.'

Several New Zealand examples of Arneis have been released in the past couple of years, from Clevedon Hills, Coopers Creek, Matawhero, Montana, Trinity Hill and Villa Maria. Of all the emerging white-wine varieties, so far Arneis is the most distinctive and promising.

If you like this wine, also try: Clevedon Hills Arneis; Matawhero Gisborne Arneis

TOHU MARLBOROUGH SAUVIGNON BLANC

TOHU (pronounced 'Tor-who') is New Zealand's first Maori-owned wine company. This is its most acclaimed wine — the 2007 and 2008 vintages won gold medals at the Air New Zealand Wine Awards; the 2010 scooped the trophy for champion Sauvignon Blanc at the 2010 Romeo Bragato Wine Awards — but that doesn't stop wine lovers around the country snapping up bottles for below $20. From one vintage to the next, it offers terrific value.

Price: $19

Maori are involved in all stages of the wine's production. Owned by Nelson-based Wakatu Incorporation, Tohu (which means 'mark' or 'sign') also has interests in commercial property, paua and crayfish, horticulture and forestry.

Tohu is no 'boutique' winery. Its CEO since 2010 has been Mike Brown — formerly chief winemaker and general manager of one of Nelson's largest and best wine producers, Waimea Estates — and its annual output is approaching 100,000 cases.

Tohu Marlborough Sauvignon Blanc flows entirely from the company's 'flagship' Upton Downs Road Vineyard, on the south bank of the Awatere River. Thirty kilometres inland, in the upper reaches of the valley — more than 200 metres above sea level — the vines are cultivated on stony river terraces at 'the extreme edge of viticulture in

Marlborough'. Yields are low, averaging 9 tonnes of grapes per hectare.

At the winery, the machine-harvested grapes are pressed gently and the juice, after a day or two of settling, is inoculated with a neutral yeast strain. It is then fermented cool in stainless steel tanks to 'retain freshness and varietal character'.

Tohu describes the 2009 vintage as having 'an intense mineral nose showcasing classic Awatere Valley characters of tomato stalk, gooseberries and lemongrass. On the palate our Sauvignon shows more herbaceous, green pepper and fleshy guava notes, with a steely minerality providing focus. Racy acidity provides a long and very crisp finish, with a touch of fruit sweetness for balance.'

The wine is unmistakably of Awatere Valley origin; those intense 'tomato stalk' aromas are an almost guaranteed giveaway. But its green, herbaceous characters are balanced by riper, passionfruit-like flavours, and the wine is impressively concentrated, vigorous, crisp and dry.

Tohu produces another, higher-priced Sauvignon Blanc. Named in honour of Blenheim kaumatua (elder) Mugwi Macdonald, Tohu Mugwi Reserve Sauvignon Blanc is a weighty, barrel-fermented style, very smooth, generous and fleshy.

BEST BUY

If you like this wine, also try: Clos Marguerite Marlborough Sauvignon Blanc; Tupari Marlborough Sauvignon Blanc

TRINITY HILL GIMBLETT GRAVELS VIOGNIER

SEDUCTIVELY weighty, rich and soft, with notable depth of peach, pear and spice flavours and the barest hint of oak, this is one of New Zealand's most acclaimed Viogniers. The 2004, 2005 and 2006 vintages collected gold medals and trophies on both sides of the Tasman, which seems entirely appropriate, given that John Hancock, the driving force behind Trinity Hill, is a South Australian who since 1979 has made increasingly innovative and exciting wines in New Zealand.

Price: $35

Hancock delights in the fact that Hawke's Bay succeeds with a wide selection of grape varieties. 'I reckon there's not another wine region in the world that can make the diversity of styles Hawke's Bay can, at the quality levels we achieve,' he told *New Zealand Winegrower*. Trinity Hill, he points out, has won gold medals for Viognier, Sauvignon Blanc, Chardonnay, Pinot Noir, Syrah, Cabernet Sauvignon, Merlot, Montepulciano and Tempranillo.

The Viognier grapes are grown in the Gimblett Gravels, at Trinity Hill's Gimblett Stones and Gimblett Estate vineyards. The fruit is harvested by hand at advanced ripeness levels (22.5 to over 27 brix) and the juice is fermented in a combination of stainless steel tanks and seasoned French oak barrels. After maturing for about three months on its yeast lees, the young wine is bottled with gentle acidity and a high level of alcohol (typically 14.5 per cent). It is basically a dry style (harbouring only 2 to 4 grams per litre of residual sugar).

Hancock and his executive winemaker, Warren Gibson (who has his own separate label, Bilancia), describe Trinity Hill Gimblett Gravels Viognier as having 'the distinct aromas and flavours of orange blossom, cumquat peel and jasmine. ... The rich, full and soft texture is the enduring feature. The exotic and sensual nature of this wine makes it ... hard not to drink!' With its lovely sweet-fruit delights and silky-smooth feel in the mouth, it slips down very easily.

Trinity Hill also produces a lower-priced Hawke's Bay Viognier, peachy, dry and well-rounded; and a lush, sweet, botrytis-enriched Noble Viognier, which can also be impossible to resist.

If you like this wine, also try: Trinity Hill Hawke's Bay Viognier; Villa Maria Cellar Selection Hawke's Bay Viognier

TUPARI AWATERE VALLEY MARLBOROUGH SAUVIGNON BLANC

TUPARI is the personal label of Glenn Thomas and his partners, David and Heather Turnbull. As you'd expect of the Awatere Valley's most experienced winemaker, the wines are immaculate.

Thomas says his vision for his own Sauvignon Blanc is a wine 'of understated elegance, with intensity of flavour and fine palate structure'. Tupari is an authoritative wine, with powerful stone-fruit and lime flavours, a minerally streak, and great presence.

Price: $29

Thomas and his partner, Sharon Inwood, arrived in the Awatere Valley in 1988, the same year as David and Heather Turnbull began farming higher in the valley. Born in England, Thomas worked in Australian wineries before he joined Corbans in Gisborne in 1986. Three years later, he produced the first wines ever to flow from the Awatere Valley: Vavasour Fume Blanc 1989 and Dashwood Sauvignon Blanc 1989.

The two couples met when Thomas and Inwood leased the Turnbulls' farm cottage. 'It only took a few bottles of wine for Glenn to convince the Turnbulls that their north-facing river terraces were ideally suited to viticulture and in 2002 Tupari vineyard was planted...'

Tupari (pronounced 'Too-par-ree') takes its name from the dramatic cliffs in the upper Awatere Valley. At 150 to 200 metres above sea level, the vineyard is in the upper reaches of the valley's grapegrowing zone. Stones under the vines 'radiate warmth long into the night, complemented by regular cooling sea breezes that flow up the valley in the late afternoon'. Yields are low, at just 6 to 8 tonnes of grapes per hectare.

At the winery, the juice is cool-fermented with cultured yeasts in stainless steel tanks, and the wine is then aged on its yeast lees for six or seven months, with weekly lees-stirring. Thomas views this extended lees contact as a key refinement. 'It results in a later release date than most Marlborough Sauvignon Blancs. However, the result is a creaminess on the palate and a wine that will retain its freshness well beyond the first year.'

Tupari Sauvignon Blanc is a powerful wine, rich and ripe, yet also minerally and racy. Weighty, concentrated and zingy, its flavours build to a lasting finish.

'Concentrated white peach and citrus flavours and a distinct mineral quality,' is how Thomas describes the wine. 'The long and creamy palate finishes with a refreshing acidity.' Experience counts. It's benchmark stuff.

If you like this wine, also try: Clos Marguerite Marlborough Sauvignon Blanc; Clos Henri Marlborough Sauvignon Blanc

VALLI OLD VINE CENTRAL OTAGO RIESLING

BONE-dry Riesling is rare in New Zealand, but if Riesling is to escape the sales doldrums, we need more *dry* wines. Which makes this authoritative wine all the more exciting.

Grant Taylor carved out a high profile during his long spell (1993–2006) as winemaker at Gibbston Valley. In 1998 he launched his own label, Valli, naming it after his great-great-grandfather, Giuseppe Valli, from an Italian winemaking background, who immigrated to New Zealand in the 1870s.

Pinot Noir is Taylor's greatest love and his Gibbston Vineyard, Bannockburn Vineyard and Waitaki Vineyard Pinot Noirs are full of interest. But he also produces 400-odd cases per year of this exceptional, very refined, intense and racy Riesling.

Price: $28

The wine's dryness and fresh acidity, says Taylor, is balanced 'by a core of concentrated, ripe fruit and depth of flavour that only old vines and low cropping levels can achieve'. He describes his Old Vine Riesling as 'aromatically very perfumed, with white peach and ripe stone-fruits, and a hint of clean, dusty, crushed rock (the minerality associated with this variety)'.

The grapes come from a 1-hectare block near Alexandra, at Black Ridge Winery. Verdun Burgess, who planted the vines in 1981, believes the schist-based soils flavour the wine. 'Riesling has a very tough root system. It can squeeze water out of a stone, and it sucks minerals out of the rock. Black Ridge flavours are especially pronounced in the Riesling.'

For Taylor, the attraction is that the vines are among the oldest in the South Island, 'and consequently have the root mass to fully ripen the fruit and add complexity from the soil'. And of all New Zealand's grapegrowing regions, Alexandra has 'the greatest diurnal temperature range, perfect for Riesling — the hot days mean the fruit really ripens, while the cool nights help retain its acidity'.

The fruit is hand-harvested in late April from very low-yielding vines (3.5 to 4 tonnes of grapes per hectare). The juice is cool-fermented in stainless steel tanks and the wine is bottled with about 13 per cent alcohol and no residual sugar.

Valli Old Vine Riesling is a deliciously rich, dry but not austere wine, capable of lengthy aging. From a block of Riesling vines at Lowburn, in the Cromwell Basin, in 2010 Valli also produced a sweet, botrytis-affected Dolce Vita Late Harvest Riesling. Taylor sees it as a wine 'only possible because of the right alignment of stars, moon, planets and who knows what else...'.

If you like this wine, also try: Rippon Riesling; Valli Dolce Vita Late Harvest Riesling

VILLA MARIA CELLAR SELECTION HAWKE'S BAY VIOGNIER

'A hidden treasure for many years is finally beginning to rear its head,' declared Villa Maria in 2009. 'The company's sales of Viognier grew 260 per cent in the last 12 months, including a whopping 350 per cent growth in domestic sales.'

The launch of the company's Private Bin East Coast Viognier the year before at only $20 had obviously boosted sales. 'Perhaps it's the French name that has previously deterred wine drinkers? Perhaps it has been the fear of the unknown? All that is in the past now...'

Price: $24

The Private Bin bottling is very good, but the Cellar Selection is the one to grab. Sold for less than $25, it has a formidable track record on the show circuit. The 2009 vintage won the trophy for champion Viognier at the 2010 Royal Easter Show Wine Awards; the 2007 won a gold medal at the 2008 Air New Zealand Wine Awards, plus the Viognier trophy at three other competitions in New Zealand — including the 2008 Royal Easter Show Wine Awards.

Fleshy and fragrant, Villa Maria Cellar Selection Hawke's Bay Viognier is a rich, creamy-textured wine with deep stone-fruit flavours, a hint of spices and a dry finish. The winemakers describe it as 'heady, with exotic aromatics, featuring honeysuckle, peach and nutmeg spice notes. The palate is unctuous with complementary spicy barrel notes providing texture, complexity and length.'

Why are the grapes grown in Hawke's Bay rather than Marlborough? 'Viognier performs best in regions with warm temperatures, high sunshine hours and low rainfall,' says Villa Maria, 'all of which are characteristics of the Hawke's Bay climate.' In other words, Marlborough is too cool.

The grapes are hand-harvested and the juice is soaked on the skins for up to six hours, to 'extract and enhance the flavour and aromatics'. A small part of the blend is handled in tanks but, in 2010, 85 per cent was fermented with selected yeasts in French barriques (15 per cent new). Post-ferment, the wine was lees-stirred weekly, with 40 per cent malolactic fermentation, 'to build layers of texture and maintain freshness'.

Villa Maria Private Bin East Coast Viognier is also well worth trying. Handled mostly in tanks, it is less rich than the Cellar Selection Hawke's Bay Viognier, but floral, vibrantly fruity, smooth and dry.

At the top of the range is the fully barrel-fermented, weighty Villa Maria Single Vineyard Omahu Gravels Hawke's Bay Viognier — a powerful, fleshy, scented wine with highly concentrated stone-fruit flavours, complex, creamy and rich. Top vintages are benchmark stuff.

If you like this wine, also try: Villa Maria Single Vineyard Omahu Gravels Hawke's Bay Viognier; Trinity Hill Gimblett Gravels Viognier

VILLA MARIA PRIVATE BIN MARLBOROUGH SAUVIGNON BLANC

IF you pay the suggested retail price for this popular wine, it'll set you back $21. Hardly anyone does. In supermarkets around the country, it's often on 'promotion' for less than $15, and can sometimes be snapped up at $11.95. At that price, it's arguably the best-value white wine on the market.

Don't be fooled by those low prices — this is an excellent wine, with a strong track record in shows to prove it. Take the 2010 vintage. Awarded a silver medal at the New Zealand International Wine Show 2010, it then scooped a gold at the New World Wine Awards 2010. The Australians rated it even more highly, awarding it the trophy for champion Sauvignon Blanc at the 2010 Royal Perth Wine Show.

Price: $12–21

Every year, this large-volume wine is a pleasure to drink. Very fresh and zingy, it offers strong melon, lime and green-capsicum flavours, dry and crisp. If you taste it alongside some of Marlborough's most prestigious, higher-priced Sauvignon Blancs, it generally holds its own well.

To obtain a range of flavours and blending options, the grapes are grown at sites across the Wairau and Awatere valleys, and picked at varying ripeness levels over a period of several weeks. To preserve the grapes' most delicate aromas and flavours, the juice is cool-fermented in tanks. Bottled early to capture its vibrancy and freshness, it is made in a basically dry style (with about 3.5 grams per litre of residual sugar to balance its appetising acidity).

Villa Maria's winemaking team describe the 2010 Private Bin as a 'powerful Sauvignon Blanc, bursting with a myriad of flavours including gooseberry, passionfruit, fresh citrus, melon and nettle-dominant herbaceous aromas'. They describe the palate as 'enticing ... with layers of juicy flavours, intensity and concentration, finishing with a refreshing, crisp, clean line of acidity'.

Villa Maria also produces several other top-flight Marlborough Sauvignon Blancs in its top-tier Reserve and Single Vineyard ranges, and a very intense and zingy, passionfruit and lime-flavoured Sauvignon Blanc in its mid-priced Cellar Selection range.

But for sheer value it's hard to beat the fresh, punchy, hugely drinkable Private Bin Marlborough Sauvignon Blanc.

BEST BUY

If you like this wine, also try: Villa Maria Cellar Selection Marlborough Sauvignon Blanc; Saint Clair Marlborough Sauvignon Blanc

VILLA MARIA SINGLE VINEYARD KELTERN CHARDONNAY

OF 14 gold medals awarded to Chardonnays at the 2010 Air New Zealand Wine Awards, eight were collected by a single company. Of Villa Maria's many Chardonnays, made from Auckland, Gisborne, Hawke's Bay and Marlborough grapes, the Single Vineyard Keltern is arguably the greatest.

Keltern is a star performer on the show circuit. The 2008 vintage won a gold medal and the trophy for champion Chardonnay at the 2010 Romeo Bragato Wine Awards. The 2007 achieved the same feat at the Bragato awards in 2009, while also scooping three other gold medals in New Zealand, plus the trophy for Champion Wine of Show at the 2010 Liquorland International Wine Competition.

Price: **$37**

Keltern Vineyard lies inland from Hastings, east of Maraekakaho, in Hawke's Bay. The vines, in an old riverbed, are planted on a warm site with deep loams overlying free-draining gravels.

For Villa Maria, the goal is a wine capable of maturing gracefully for five to seven years. The 2009 vintage, it says, is 'very restrained and elegant . . . [with] a fragrant bouquet, displaying toast and grapefruit aromas, complemented by complex notes of flint, limes and grilled nut. A tightly woven palate unfolds, displaying seamless integration and genuine length.'

The grapes are hand-picked and the juice is run straight to French oak barriques (35 per cent to 50 per cent new). In some vintages (such as 2007) it is fermented with natural yeasts; in others with cultured yeasts (2008); in others with both (2009).

The proportion of the blend that undergoes a softening malolactic fermentation also varies, from 50 per cent to 100 per cent. Post-ferment, the wine spends a further 10 months on its yeast lees, with weekly *batonnage* (stirring of its yeast lees) to 'help build palate texture and richness'.

Villa Maria also produces impressive Single Vineyard Chardonnays from Ihumatao — its headquarters at Mangere, in South Auckland — and Taylors Pass, in Marlborough; superb regional Chardonnays from Gisborne, Hawke's Bay and Marlborough under its Reserve label; and affordable, fine-value Chardonnays under its middle-tier Cellar Selection label and 'commercial' Private Bin East Coast label.

Top vintages of the Single Vineyard Keltern Chardonnay are exceptionally powerful and 'complete', offering generous, highly concentrated stone-fruit flavours and a creamy-smooth texture.

If you like this wine, also try: Villa Maria Single Vineyard Ihumatao Chardonnay; Mission Jewelstone Chardonnay

VILLA MARIA SINGLE VINEYARD SEDDON PINOT GRIS

ONE of the highlights of Villa Maria's extensive range is its gloriously scented, very fresh and rich Single Vineyard Seddon Pinot Gris, which ranks among the country's greatest examples of the classic Alsace variety.

'*Terroir* wines, reflecting the unique vineyard sites from which they come,' is how Sir George Fistonich, the founder of Villa Maria, sums up his company's Single Vineyard range. In the winery, he encourages his staff to adopt a non-interventional approach, 'allowing the wine to take its own path and express its own distinct personality'.

Price: $32

The Single Vineyard range, launched in 2003, at last count featured more than 20 wines. While Villa Maria's other top-tier selection, labelled Reserve, celebrates regional styles, blended from various high-performing vineyards, the Single Vineyard range narrows the focus to specific sites.

Pinot Gris grows well in New Zealand, says company viticulturist Oliver Powrie. After experimenting with various sites, 'we've been able to select some fantastic vineyards which are beginning to produce fruit of exceptional quality'.

None more than Seddon Vineyard, perched high on the southern bank of Marlborough's Awatere

River. An exposed river terrace, it is a warm site, cooled by evening winds off the slopes of Mt Tapuae-o-Uenuku.

The low-yielding vines, exposed to wind throughout the year, are grown in free-draining, sandy silt loams, overlying aged gravels. Trained on a vertical shoot-positioned trellis, they are leaf-plucked around the bunch zone to enhance the ripening grapes' exposure to sunshine. 'As a direct result of this particular site and viticultural management,' reports Villa Maria, 'the vines produce very small-berried bunches with intensely concentrated flavours.'

The Single Vineyard Seddon Pinot Gris is cool-fermented in a mix of stainless steel tanks (mostly) and seasoned French oak barriques. It is then matured for several months on its yeast lees, with weekly *batonnage* (stirring.)

A powerful, sturdy wine, the Single Vineyard Seddon Pinot Gris is floral and buoyantly fruity, with a slightly oily texture. It offers notably concentrated, lush flavours of pears, lychees and spices, with a long, dryish finish.

The Single Vineyard Seddon label is just one of four Pinot Gris under the Villa Maria brand. Also worth discovering is the Single Vineyard Seddon Pinot Noir, a notably refined, deliciously concentrated, savoury and supple red.

If you like this wine, also try: Villa Maria Cellar Selection Marlborough Pinot Gris; Villa Maria Single Vineyard Seddon Pinot Noir

VINOPTIMA ORMOND RESERVE GEWÜRZTRAMINER

>>>

A quick look at its website will leave you in absolutely no doubt about the goal of this small Gisborne winery: Vinoptima is a true specialist, 'dedicated to producing the world's best Gewürztraminer'. Since the first wine flowed in 2003, only four vintages have been released, but the results have been spectacular.

Price: $85–90

Top vintages of Vinoptima ('best wine') are weighty, concentrated and full of personality, showing outstanding richness, complexity and harmony. It is often compared favourably with *grand cru* Alsace Gewürztraminers.

Nick Nobilo, the driving force behind Vinoptima, believes Gewürztraminer is underrated. 'To me, Gewürztraminer is one of the most noble grape varieties and when produced faithfully, it can be one of the world's great wine styles.' It has an intriguing personality. 'It can display immense fruit sweetness yet finish quite dry, bordering on being bitter, but then dissolve in the aftertaste into most complex and exotic flavours unseen in any other white variety.'

One of three brothers who for decades ran Nobilo — now owned by US-based wine giant

Constellation Brands — in West Auckland, Nick was highly acclaimed as a winemaker during the 1970s, pioneering such classic red-wine varieties as Cabernet Sauvignon, while also popularising Müller-Thurgau. During the 1980s and early 1990s, he was Nobilo's ambitious, export-focused chief executive.

At Vinoptima, Nick Nobilo wanted a single-variety vineyard with its own on-site winery. 'Everything — right from the growing of the grapes to the making of the wine and the bottling — is done on the estate.'

The 10-hectare vineyard at Ormond lies on a warm, inland site — 26 kilometres from the coast — with rich, alluvial clay soils. The grapes are harvested by hand at an advanced stage of ripeness (in 2009, from 24.5 to 26.5 brix), and the juice is fermented in a combination of stainless steel tanks and large, 1200-litre German oak ovals.

In favourable seasons, Vinoptima also makes a memorable Gewürztraminer Noble Late Harvest. Harvested in early winter, the debut 2004 vintage is a magical wine: honey-sweet but not at all cloying, with wonderful depth and personality.

If you like this wine, also try: Vinoptima Ormond Gewürztraminer Noble Late Harvest; Johanneshof Marlborough Gewürztraminer

WAIMEA CLASSIC NELSON RIESLING

THIS is no shy creature, revealing its secrets over years, even decades. 'The idea behind the Classic Riesling,' according to Waimea Estates, is to make a wine 'with personality and upfront appeal, by combining citrus elements with tropical-fruit and honeyed characters.'

Always a top buy, this lush, full-flavoured Nelson Riesling is very skilfully balanced for early drinking. With its lively acidity, distinct splash of sweetness, hint of honey, and fresh, intense lemon/lime flavours, it is typically a lovely mouthful.

Price: **$18**

Waimea Estates, owned by Trevor and Robyn Bolitho, is one of Nelson's largest wineries. Its 140 hectares of vineyards are planted in a wide array of grapes. The key varieties are Sauvignon Blanc, Pinot Noir, Pinot Gris, Chardonnay — and Riesling.

The vines for the Classic Riesling are estate-grown on the Waimea Plains, south-west of Nelson city, in free-draining, alluvial soils. Late-harvested fruit adds 'a subtle nuance of honeyed botrytis to the wine'.

The grapes are harvested in the cool, early morning 'to protect their delicate aromatics', and the juice is given a long, cool fermentation with cultured yeasts in stainless steel tanks. When the residual sugar is deemed to be in balance with the acidity, the fermentation is arrested by chilling.

Waimea Classic Riesling is produced in a medium to medium-dry style (varying with the season), with mouth-watering acidity to keep everything lively. Judges love it. The 2003 won gold medals at the New World Wine Awards 2005 and the Bragato Wine Awards 2005. The 2009 vintage scooped a gold medal at the Air New Zealand Wine Awards 2010, together with trophies at the New Zealand International Wine Show 2010 and International Aromatic Wine Competition 2010.

If you are a Riesling fan, Waimea Estates makes several other Rieslings — a tight, lemony, appley, minerally Dry Riesling; a rich, ripe, peachy, gently honeyed Bolitho SV Riesling; a gently sweet Late Harvest Riesling; an amber-hued, honey-sweet, treacly Bolitho SV Noble Riesling; and a good-value, easy-drinking, medium-dry Riesling under its low-priced Spinyback brand.

BEST BUY

WAIMEA
classic riesling
NELSON

If you like this wine, also try: Waimea Bolitho SV Nelson Riesling; Framingham Classic Marlborough Riesling

〈〈〈

WAIMEA NELSON PINOT GRIS

OF the several hundred New Zealand Pinot Gris now on the market, I can't think of any label with a better claim to be the 'best buy', from one vintage to the next, than this Nelson beauty. Deliciously full-bodied, it's a medium-dry style, soft and rich. A powerful Pinot Gris in the classic Alsace mould, it is fleshy and ripely perfumed, with a slightly oily texture and deep stone-fruit and spice flavours.

Price: **$22**

Nelson's second-largest producer (after Seifried Estate), Waimea Estates is owned by Trevor and Robyn Bolitho, who were orchardists for many years before planting their first vines in 1993. They now control 140 hectares of vines — mostly Sauvignon Blanc, Pinot Noir, Pinot Gris, Riesling and Chardonnay — on the Waimea Plains, and enjoy a particularly strong reputation for aromatic white wines.

Winemaker Trudy Sheild has worked at Domaine Bott-Geyl, a respected Alsace producer of Pinot Gris, Gewürztraminer and Riesling. In New Zealand, she says, the emerging style of Pinot Gris 'is fruit-driven and is often as much about texture as flavour — all achieved by cool ferments in stainless steel followed by some lees contact. Significant levels of residual sugar not only bolster the fruit but contribute to this easy-drinking style.'

At Waimea Estates, Trudy says, the goal with Pinot

Gris is a wine with 'a delicate aroma of pears, apples and honeysuckle, through to stone-fruit, with yeasty, biscuity nuances, and a soft, nicely textured palate.'

The grapes are hand-picked from the company's vines, grown in stony, alluvial soils, at an advanced ripeness level of about 24 brix. The fermentation, conducted at moderately cool temperatures in stainless steel tanks, is stopped to retain residual sugar, and the yeast lees are stirred twice-weekly for several months 'to add a savoury, mealy note, plus structure and texture to the palate'.

The result is a hard-to-resist, weighty wine (typically 14.5 per cent alcohol), very generous and concentrated, with a gentle splash of sweetness and a rich, rounded mouthfeel. Who said fine Pinot Gris had to be expensive?

There has been no shortage of accolades. The 2005 vintage scooped five-star awards in *Winestate* and *Cuisine*; the 2008 won a gold medal at the 2009 *Decanter* World Wine Awards.

Two other Pinot Gris from Waimea Estates are worth discovering. Waimea Bolitho SV Pinot Gris (SV stands for Signature Vineyard) is a sweeter style with gentle acidity and rich, ripe flavours, lush and soft.

Spinyback Nelson Pinot Gris, the driest of the trio, is another consistently good buy; the 2008 vintage won the international trophy for Best White Single Varietal, under £10, at the *Decanter* World Wine Awards 2009.

BEST BUY

WAIMEA
pinot gris
NELSON
NEW ZEALAND WINE

If you like this wine, also try: Spinyback Nelson Pinot Gris; Waimea Nelson Gewürztraminer

SWEET

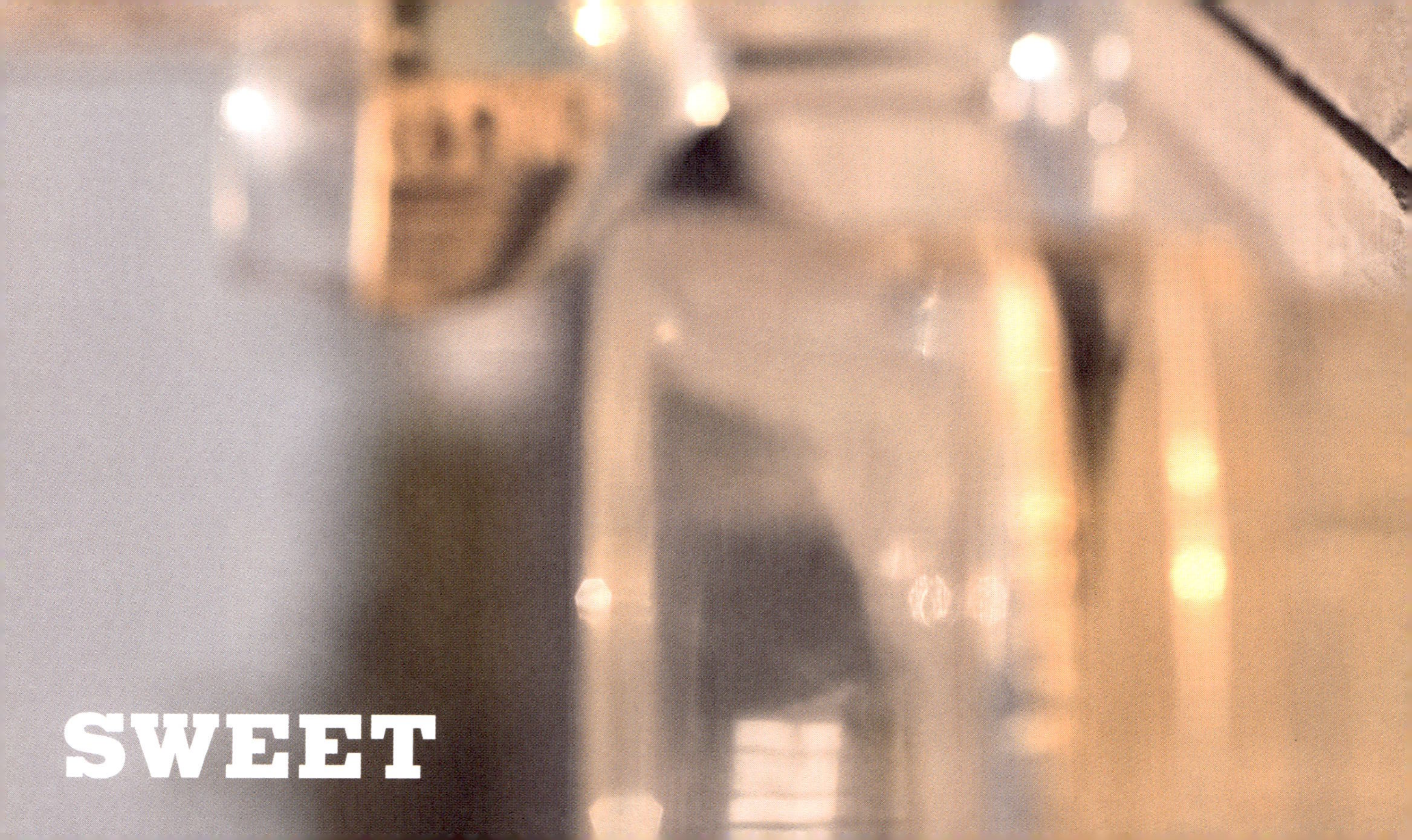

CHURCH ROAD RESERVE NOBLE VIOGNIER

CHURCH Road makes a top-flight Reserve Hawke's Bay Viognier — concentrated, peachy and creamy. Deliciously rich, soft and dry, it's hard to resist, but this sweet version is *impossible* to resist.

Winemaker Chris Scott notes that Viognier is still a fairly recent arrival in Hawke's Bay, 'and we have been progressively learning more about this exciting, full-bodied, aromatic white grape since our first harvest in 2004. While we had been targeting a dry style, we noticed that the variety had a good propensity to develop "noble rot" late in the season, once the fruit was very ripe. ... The typical strong apricot, citrus and floral aromas of the variety are present, along with honeyed and slightly nutty notes that come from the botrytis itself.'

Price: $36 (375ML)

The grapes are grown at two sites owned by Pernod Ricard NZ: the Korokipo Vineyard, between Taradale and Fernhill, where the vines are established in silt loam soils; and the Redstone Vineyard, in The Triangle, planted in shallow, light silts over reddish gravels.

The Viognier fruit is harvested by hand during April and early May with soaring sugar levels (35 to 50 brix).

At the historic Church Road Winery at Taradale, the debut 2008 vintage was fermented in a 50:50 split of tanks and French oak barriques; the 2009 was wholly tank-fermented. The wine is bottled with a moderate alcohol level (11 to 12.5 per cent) and abundant sweetness (up 240 grams per litre of residual sugar).

Delicious in its youth, the Reserve Noble Viognier offers lush stone-fruit, spice and honey flavours, showing lovely intensity and harmony. The style is described vividly by Scott: 'On the nose, the wine shows opulent honeysuckle, orange blossom and dried apricot, along with honeyed and nutty aromas. The palate is full-bodied, almost viscous [syrupy], with an intense sweetness balanced by a citrus acidity.'

The 2009 vintage won a gold medal and the trophy for champion sweet wine at the 2010 Hawke's Bay A & P Mercedes-Benz Wine Awards. Church Road suggests serving it as an apéritif, with strong cheeses, nuts, dried fruits and pâté; or as a dessert wine, with creamy, rather than overtly sweet, dishes.

Or you can just savour this magical wine by itself. Delectably scented, sweet and soft, it's very 'complete'.

If you like this wine, also try: Trinity Hill Hawke's Bay Noble Viognier; Millton Clos Samuel Viognier Special Bunch Selection

FORREST ESTATE BOTRYTISED RIESLING

GREAT dessert wines are a labour of love in combination with a lot of good luck,' believes winemaker John Forrest. He makes a fresh, elegant Late Harvest Riesling and Late Harvest Gewürztraminer, but the star of Forrest Estate's sweet-wine trio is the breathtakingly beautiful Botrytised Riesling.

In a region saturated with Sauvignon Blanc, Forrest is adamant that Riesling is the premier variety. 'Riesling shows a tremendous affinity for the *terroir* of Marlborough, benefiting from the wonderfully long, dry, cool autumns.' He has picked Riesling from as early as late March to as late as mid-June, producing a diversity of styles. 'All have those quintessential Riesling characters of fruit intensity and natural acidity.'

Price: $35 (375ML)

The Botrytised Riesling is rich and finely poised, with lush fruit flavours enriched but not swamped by botrytis and enlivened by racy acidity. 'I want an oily, unctuous wine,' says Forrest, 'with pure, orange marmalade fruit characters and a clean acid finish on the palate.'

The key challenge when making dessert wines is to get the grapes fully ripe while it is still warm enough for botrytis to spread. 'You need completely ripe, not green-edged, fruit that has matured to orange marmalade flavours,' says Forrest. 'If it's warm and moist during mid-April, botrytis invades the ripe grapes, but if it doesn't happen by 20 April, it's all over — it's too cool for the botrytis to spread.'

To give botrytis a helping hand, long grass is grown between the rows and sprinkled with water in the morning. 'By wetting the vineyard environment, we can get the humidity to rise, which encourages the spread of botrytis,' says Forrest.

The grapes are hand-picked from early May to early June, at advanced ripeness levels (28 to 44 brix), and the juice is cool-fermented with cultured yeasts in stainless steel tanks. Once the desired balance of sugar and acidity has been achieved, the ferment is arrested and the wine is bottled young, with low alcohol (typically 9 per cent), mouth-watering acidity and abundant sweetness (around 200 grams per litre of residual sugar).

Forrest Estate Botrytised Riesling is highly scented and poised, with luscious, sweet honey and apricot flavours. This delectable wine is a star of the show circuit. If you try it, you'll see why.

If you like this wine, also try: Villa Maria Reserve Noble Riesling; Pegasus Bay Aria Late Harvest Riesling

SPARKLING

DEUTZ MARLBOROUGH CUVÉE BLANC DE BLANCS

THE flagship sparkling from Pernod Ricard NZ, formerly Montana, is its popular Deutz Marlborough Cuvée Brut NV. But this rarer, higher-priced bubbly, Chardonnay-based and vintage-dated, is even finer.

Sparkling wines under the Deutz brand have been produced in New Zealand since 1988, under an agreement between Pernod Ricard NZ and its forerunners, and the Champagne house of Deutz, a top Champagne house, owned by Roederer. One of the largest independent houses, Louis Roederer has been controlled by the same family since it was founded in 1776.

Price: $40

Launched as a non-vintage style in 1993, Deutz Marlborough Cuvée Blanc de Blancs has been vintage-dated since the 1990 vintage was released in 1995. A star of the show circuit, it has been awarded more top accolades of late than any other sparkling. The 2006 vintage won five trophies. At the 2009 Air New Zealand Wine Awards, where it scooped the trophy for champion sparkling, the judges commented: 'It's stylish and complex, showing floral and yeasty flavours with an exquisitely fine mouthfeel. Simply stunning.'

The grapes are grown in the Wairau Valley, in

the company's silty, stony Renwick Estate, and in more clay-based soils in the Brancott Vineyard. Harvested by hand, the grapes are pressed in a computer-controlled French Champagne press, which yields juice of great delicacy. The various batches of base wine are kept separate during the initial alcoholic fermentation, and left on their yeast lees while undergoing a malolactic fermentation. After the *assemblage*, the final blend is bottled for its secondary, bubble-inducing fermentation, and is then matured on its yeast lees in the bottle for up to three years before it is disgorged.

Winemaker Julia O'Connell says the Blanc de Blancs displays 'aromas of almonds, toast and lemon zest. Intense lemon sorbet dominates the mid-palate, along with complex secondary yeast autolysis flavours of toast, almonds, freshly baked bread and biscuit flavours.'

Typically a very piercing and racy wine, Deutz Marlborough Cuvée Blanc de Blancs has lovely delicacy and depth of vibrant, citrusy, yeasty, nutty flavours, with a long, slightly creamy finish. The Deutz Marlborough Cuvée range also includes the intense, yeasty Brut NV; a strawberry and spice-flavoured Rosé NV that shows excellent lightness and vivacity; and a distinguished Prestige Cuvée, disgorged after three and a half years on its yeast lees, revealing outstanding richness and complexity.

If you like this wine, also try: Deutz Marlborough Cuvée Brut NV; Nautilus Cuvée Marlborough

LINDAUER BRUT CUVÉE

>>> ONE Saturday evening, I spent half an hour in a supermarket wine department, observing what people were buying. Every second customer headed straight to the fridge and grabbed a chilled bottle of Lindauer.

A three and a half-star wine at a two-star price, Lindauer Brut Cuvée (usually just called Lindauer) has a recommended retail price of $16, but you can often pick up a bottle in supermarkets for $10 or less. Yet it is typically lively and lemony, slightly yeasty and nutty, showing far greater complexity and richness than you'd expect for such a low-priced bubbly.

Price: **$8–16**

Launched by Montana in 1981 in Brut (dry) and Sec (medium) versions, Lindauer was the country's first readily available bottle-fermented bubbly. Named after the Bohemian artist Gottfried Lindauer, who emigrated to New Zealand in 1874, it was an instant success. For countless Kiwis, it was unthinkable to party without Lindauer.

By 2000, New Zealanders were drinking more than three million bottles of Lindauer per year, and more Lindauer was exported, especially to the UK, than any other New Zealand wine. If Lindauer had been a company in its own right, it would have ranked as New Zealand's third-largest winery.

Over the years, the Lindauer recipe has changed, in terms of grape varieties and regions. The first batches were based on Gisborne Pinot Noir. A decade later, Lindauer was a blend of Pinot

Noir (45 per cent), Chardonnay (25 per cent), Chenin Blanc (15 per cent) and Riesling (15 per cent), grown in Gisborne and Marlborough. By 2007, it had evolved into a blend of Chardonnay (60 per cent) and Pinot Noir (40 per cent), sourced from Gisborne and Hawke's Bay.

The period Lindauer spends maturing on its yeast lees has also changed, from 18 months in 1993 to 15 months by 2004, and lately to a year. Yet Lindauer has stayed a reliably good drop — full-flavoured, vivacious and balanced for easy, satisfying drinking.

In 2010, Pernod Ricard NZ sold Lindauer and other brands to a joint venture by brewer Lion Nathan and Indevin, New Zealand's largest independent contract winemaker. The wine is now made by Indevin, for distribution by Lion Nathan.

Will Lindauer's reputation for good quality and exceptional value survive the changes? Karl du Fresne, in the *NZ Listener* (19–25 February 2011), says 'it's now rumoured the new owners of Lindauer will stop making it by the bottle-fermentation method and instead use the much cheaper, and inferior, tank-fermentation process'.

The sample I tasted in August 2010 was even better than expected — highly fragrant, with strong, yeasty flavours. If Indevin's winemakers can match the standard set by Pernod Ricard NZ, Lindauer should enjoy another 30 years of runaway popularity.

BEST BUY

If you like this wine, also try: Lindauer Special Reserve Brut Cuvée; Morton Premium Brut

NAUTILUS CUVÉE MARLBOROUGH

IT was inevitable that Nautilus Estate, owned by one of the country's top wine distributors, Negociants NZ, would plunge into the production of fine sparkling wine. Negociants itself is a subsidiary of S. Smith & Son, owned by the Hill-Smith family, which also owns Australia's oldest family-owned winery, Yalumba — producer of the hugely popular bubbly, Angas Brut.

The base wines for Nautilus Cuvée Marlborough were first laid down in 1991. 'Apart from the obvious potential for quality sparkling wine, apparent from the few established producers,' the company declared, 'the consistently high sugar content [in the grapes] relative to the high acid and low pH also pointed to quality sparkling wine.'

Price: $39

Today, this non-vintage, Champagne-style sparkling is a blend of Pinot Noir (75 per cent) and Chardonnay (25 per cent), disgorged after a minimum of three years' lees-aging with its fruit characters subjugated by intense, bready, yeasty aromas and flavours. Lean and crisp, piercing and long, it's beautifully tight, vivacious and refined.

The style goal for Nautilus Cuvée Marlborough, says winemaker Clive Jones, is 'a sparkling wine that combines richness with finesse'. He sees Marlborough's climate as a key quality factor, with the Pinot Noir contributing 'richness and structure', Chardonnay adding 'fruit lift', and the time *en tirage* (in the bottle in contact with the yeast sediment) giving 'complexity'.

The grapes are hand-harvested at three sites in the Wairau Valley and only the best, most delicate juice is kept for the Cuvée. The individual base wines are tank-fermented with a selected Champagne yeast and then left on their yeast lees to undergo a softening malolactic fermentation. The wine is then blended and bottled to undergo its secondary fermentation.

Disgorged after three years, Nautilus Cuvée Marlborough spends an unusually long time on its yeast lees, which gives the wine its standout complexity, coupled with the addition (up to 15 per cent of the final blend) of reserve wines held in old oak. Held for six months 'on cork' before release, it has a low level of residual sugar (6 grams per litre), making it a basically dry style.

Nautilus Cuvée Marlborough has many prizes under its belt, including a blue-gold medal at the Sydney International Wine Competition in 2010.

Intensity and refinement are its hallmarks. Yeasty and nutty on the nose and palate, it's a high-flavoured, deliciously intense wine with lovely balance and a tight, harmonious, lingering finish.

If you like this wine, also try: Deutz Marlborough Cuvée Blanc de Blancs; Quartz Reef Méthode Traditionnelle Vintage

PELORUS (Vintage)

BUBBLY is hardly the first wine that springs to most wine lovers' minds in connection with Cloudy Bay. Yet the illustrious producer of Sauvignon Blanc also makes a rich, flavour-crammed, vintage-dated bubbly which for over two decades has ranked among New Zealand's few exceptional sparklings.

Pelorus is arrestingly bold, fruity and creamy — a far cry from some of the region's leaner, flintier wines. Powerful, lush and opulent, Pelorus expresses Marlborough's rich, vibrant fruit flavours, overlaid with nutty, toasty, yeasty characters. It's an exciting mouthful, explosively flavoured.

Price: $45

David Hohnen, the Australian who founded Cloudy Bay in 1985, a year later invited Harold Osborne, his former classmate at Fresno State University, to assess the scope for sparkling-wine production in Marlborough. Osborne, then working for Maison Deutz in California, visited the region, liked what he saw, and in 1987 Pelorus was born. Today, Cloudy Bay is part of the Moét-Hennessy Louis Vuitton luxury goods group, which also includes Moét & Chandon, Veuve Clicquot, Krug and Chateau d'Yquem.

Named after Pelorus Jack, the dolphin which for many years accompanied the Wellington to Nelson ferry at the mouth of Pelorus Sound, Pelorus is a less steely, much softer and fruitier style of bubbly than the traditional Champagnes of France. Vintage-dated, it is a blend of the classic Champagne grapes, Pinot Noir and Chardonnay, with always a slightly higher Pinot Noir content than Chardonnay.

The 2006 vintage was made from 10 Pinot Noir clones and five Chardonnay clones. After a primary alcoholic fermentation (partly with natural yeasts) in a mix of tanks, large vats and French oak barriques, followed by a softening malolactic fermentation and lengthy aging of the base wines prior to blending, it was bottled and matured for three years on its yeast lees, then disgorged in early 2010.

In 1998 the Chardonnay-predominant Pelorus NV was launched. A fresh, lively, crisp and appley wine, designed as an apéritif style, it is matured on its yeast lees for two years (rather than three for the vintage). A delicious wine in its own right, the non-vintage is less powerful than the vintage-dated Pelorus, which has the richness and complexity to be served at the dinner table.

Cloudy Bay describes its 2006 vintage as showing 'rich and complex aromas of brioche, nougat and almond biscotti, overlying subtle red apple and citrus fruit. The wine has a deliciously creamy structure that is balanced and focused by a fine acid backbone.' A more elegant, less bold and buttery style than some earlier releases, it is yeasty, nutty, crisp and lasting.

If you like this wine, also try: Pelorus NV; Nautilus Cuvée Marlborough

QUARTZ REEF MÉTHODE TRADITIONNELLE (Vintage)

SPECULATION has been rife for many years that Central Otago's cool climate for viticulture and high-acid grapes suit sparkling wine production. A few companies, notably Rippon and Amisfield, have released highly promising bottles of fizz, but the clear leader is Quartz Reef.

Price: $40

Highly refined, the vintage bottling of Quartz Reef Méthode Traditionnelle is distinctly Champagne-like, with lovely freshness, intensity and vivacity. Rich, lemony, yeasty and nutty, it ranks among New Zealand's greatest sparklings.

Rudi Bauer, the driving force behind Quartz Reef, was previously winemaker at Rippon Vineyard (1989–92) and Giesen Wine Estate (1992–97). His original partner in Quartz Reef — established to produce Pinot Noir, Pinot Gris and sparkling wine — was Clotilde Chauvet, who belongs to a family which owns the small Champagne house of Marc Chauvet. The partners' first bubblies were marketed as 'Quartz Reef Chauvet', but in 2008 Clotilde Chauvet withdrew from the company.

The grapes are grown at Bendigo, at a site adjacent to Quartz Reef's original Bendigo Estate

Vineyard, planted since 1998. The newer vineyard, purchased in 2008, is on a moderate, north-facing slope with sandy loam soils. It also supplies grapes for Quartz Reef's highly regarded, dry Pinot Gris, but is mostly dedicated to sparkling wine production.

From one vintage to the next, the wine's varietal composition changes. The debut 1998, 2000 and 2006 vintages have all been Chardonnay-predominant, with minor portions of Pinot Noir, but the 2001 and 2002 were both Pinot Noir-based, with smaller amounts of Chardonnay. However, the wine always spends about four years — an exceptionally long period — on its yeast lees before it is riddled and disgorged by hand. The 2006 vintage was disgorged in September 2010.

Bauer describes his classy bubbly as 'focused, fresh and crisp, with beautiful balance and length'. On the palate, it is 'creamy, textural and precise, with delightful elegance'. He also produces a lower-priced, but increasingly stylish, non-vintage sparkling, at its best very tight-knit and racy; and since 2010 a pink, strawberryish Méthode Traditionnelle Rosé.

If you like this wine, also try: Quartz Reef Méthode Traditionnelle NV; Deutz Marlborough Cuvée Blanc de Blancs

SOLJANS FUSION SPARKLING MUSCAT

≫ **FUSION** is New Zealand's closest lookalike to that famous, immensely gulpable, grapey-sweet Italian bubbly, Asti Spumante. Made from Muscat grapes grown in Gisborne, it's a deliciously light, low-alcohol wine, crisp and lively, with fresh, intense flavours, lemony, appley, zesty and vivacious.

Wines like this struggle to stand out on the show circuit, where the judges are more likely to be searching for sparklings designed in the classic Champagne mould. But that hasn't stopped Fusion Sparkling Muscat collecting a swag of silver medals, a gold medal at the Royal Easter Show Wine Awards 2009, and a gold medal and trophy at the 2004 Australian Small Winemakers Competition.

Price: $16

Tony Soljan, the owner of this small winery at Kumeu, in West Auckland, for many years offered a contract winemaking service, putting the finishing touches on sparklings made by other producers. Mark Compton, who until recently held the winemaking reins at Soljans, following well over a decade at De Redcliffe Estates, many years ago worked for Montana, where he was responsible for the bottling and production of another bubbly — Lindauer.

Based on Muscat Dr Hogg grapes, Fusion is a light, unabashedly sweet style, harbouring only 8 per cent alcohol, with 80 grams per litre of residual sugar. Once the grapes have been crushed and pressed, the juice is cold-fermented in stainless steel tanks (using the method the Italians call *metodo charmat*), which Soljans says 'helps retain the fresh fruitiness that this wine imparts'.

Soljans bottles this perfumed and frothy, seductively sweet and soft sparkling in 750-ml bottles and 1.5-litre magnums. And 'because we just love bubbles', the team also makes a lively, berryish, gently sweet Fusion Sparkling Rosé and a stylish, richly flavoured, dry Legacy Méthode Traditionnelle, based on Pinot Noir and Chardonnay, grown in Marlborough.

So when do you drink such a musky, intensely fruity, sweet and smooth wine as Fusion Sparkling Muscat? Tony Soljan serves it chilled with salads, garlic prawns, pasta and chicken dishes, or with fresh fruit salad. It's fun by itself, too.

BEST BUY

If you like this wine, also try: Soljans Fusion Sparkling Rosé; Bernadino Spumante

〈〈〈

ROSÉ

ESK VALLEY
MERLOT/MALBEC ROSÉ

>> WHAT'S in a name? Would a wine labelled rosé (French for 'pinkish') by any other name smell as sweet or taste as charming?

Rosé — now more popular in France than white wine — is ideal for the great New Zealand outdoors. Well over 100 labels are on the shelves, based mainly on Merlot in the North Island and Pinot Noir in the south.

Esk Valley, the source of New Zealand's most acclaimed rosé, has made pink wine for 20 years. 'Anyone who has visited southern Europe will know the importance given to rosé as a summer dining wine,' winemaker Gordon Russell noted in 1998. 'To sit outdoors and enjoy a chilled bottle of rosé with smoked fish or meats is one of life's great pleasures.'

Price: $24

When the 2006 vintage from Esk Valley won the trophy for champion rosé at that year's Air New Zealand Wine Awards, it was only the third time in 15 years the trophy had been awarded — and on each occasion the recipient had been Esk Valley. Since then, the accolades have kept flowing.

The grapes are grown around the Hawke's Bay region. Rosé is typically seen as a no-fuss, easy-drinking summer wine, but Russell says it is hard to make well. 'Our rosé is created from the same Merlot and Malbec grapes that are crafted into our red wines. Prior to the fermentation of the red wine, when the skins have coloured the juice sufficiently, our cellarhands lift a heavy cylindrical sieve from fermenter to fermenter, massaging it slowly into the grapes to extract up to 10 per cent of the juice.'

The pink juice is then cool-fermented like a white wine in stainless steel tanks, to capture its fresh, vibrant, red-fruit flavours. The ferment is stopped just short of dryness, leaving a whisker of residual sugar (about 4 grams per litre), and the wine is bottled as soon as possible.

It may be a challenge to make, but Esk Valley Merlot/Malbec Rosé is dead easy to drink. Full-bodied, with fresh, enticing scents, it has generous red-berry and plum flavours, slightly spicy, dryish and lively.

Whether you see rosé as a tinted white or an ultra-light red, most veer a lot closer to white than red wine in terms of basic style. When buying rosé, always go for the youngest vintage. Freshness is the essence of its appeal.

'If any wine in our range has a smile factor,' says Russell, 'it has to be the rosé.' A top picnic wine, it's a perfect partner for salmon.

If you like this wine, also try: Amisfield Saignée Rosé; Cable Bay Waiheke Island Rosé

RED

ALLUVIALE

DENSELY coloured and finely fragrant, this Hawke's Bay red is strikingly full-bodied and concentrated in a rich, Bordeaux-like style that couples power and elegance. Fully a match for many higher-priced wines, it's a steal at $30.

Kate Galloway, a Kiwi, and her French partner, David Ramonteu, are the couple behind this highly characterful blend. Galloway, who is also the winemaker for Alpha Domus — one of the best-known wineries in The

Price: **$30**

Triangle — has worked in several French wine regions. After growing up in the Pyrénées, where his family has an estate in Jurançon, Ramonteu studied at Bordeaux University, where he graduated in 1998 with a master's degree in viticulture and oenology. He now works as a winemaking consultant, with special expertise in the areas of micro-oxygenation and *élevage* (maturing wine).

The Alluviale story begins with Californian Mark Blake, who set out in 2000 to produce a single-vineyard, Bordeaux-style red in the Gimblett Gravels. Blake sold his initial 2003 vintage under a second-tier label, Alluviale, followed in 2004 by the first wine under Blake Family Vineyard's top label, Redd Gravels. However, the 2007 vintage of Redd Gravels was the last. The vineyard was sold and the Alluviale brand was snapped up by Galloway and Ramonteu (who had consulted to Mark Blake). After five vintages of Alluviale (2003–07) from Blake Family Vineyard, the couple's own first release flowed from 2008.

Alluviale is grown at two sites in Gimblett Road, in the heart of the Gimblett Gravels. It is typically Merlot-dominant, but the exact composition of the blend varies from year to year. The 2007 is a blend of Merlot and Cabernet Franc; the 2008 is a marriage of Merlot (55 per cent), Cabernet Sauvignon (25 per cent) and Cabernet Franc (20 per cent). Cabernet Sauvignon, the partners believe, gives 'a more complex and elegant style'.

New oak is definitely part of the recipe. The 2007 and 2008 vintages both spent 16 months in French oak barriques (90 per cent new).

Galloway and Ramonteu describe their sturdy, flavour-packed red as having a 'lifted aroma of damson plum, bramble, violet and roasted coffee'. The palate is complex, 'with cassis, prune and red berries, spicy oak and velvety tannins'. Dense, ripe and concentrated, it's a bold, generous red with a powerful presence.

The couple also makes a weighty, far more restrained blend of Sauvignon Blanc and Sémillon, partly barrel-fermented, called Alluviale Blanc.

BEST BUY

2008
ALLUVIALE
GIMBLETT ROAD
HAWKES BAY
NEW ZEALAND
MERLOT
RED WINE CABERNET SAUVIGNON
CABERNET FRANC

If you like this wine, also try: Clearview Enigma; Craggy Range Gimblett Gravels Merlot

ATA RANGI PINOT NOIR

AN aristocratic marriage of power and finesse, magnificently fragrant and rich, Ata Rangi is one of the finest — arguably *the* finest — of all New Zealand Pinot Noirs. Past vintages won a pile of medals and trophies, but the wine is no longer entered in local competitions. 'With the styles we want to achieve, our focus is recognition in the international arena, rather than just in New Zealand,' says Clive Paton, founder of the small Martinborough winery.

Price: **$75**

'Intense, opulent fruit with power beneath' is the style Paton is after. 'I want firmness and intense fruit. Complexity comes with time. We put enough things in there to make sure it happens. The clonal mix ensures it ages well to "forest floor" characters' (or what an Ata Rangi blurb called 'that funky, wildly sensuous, snuffly, truffly, in-the-barnyard carry-on that is the quintessence of great Pinot Noir!').

Paton got his original vines from Malcolm Abel, founder of the long-defunct Abel & Co winery at Kumeu. 'When Malcolm was still a customs officer, a vine was confiscated from a guy who'd hopped over the fence at Romanée-Conti [the fabled *grand cru* of Vosne-Romanée], taken a cutting and hidden it in his gumboot. Malcolm got the first vines out of quarantine.' That the main clone at Ata Rangi remains unidentified doesn't worry Paton: 'We know what it can do. It gives staying power and elegance.'

The grapes, harvested by hand from vines ranging from 10 to over 30 years old, are hand-sorted. The juice is fermented with natural yeasts and the wine is matured for up to a year in French oak barriques (about 25 per cent new, to avoid obvious wood characters).

Ata Rangi also produces a lower-priced but still impressive Crimson Pinot Noir, designed for early enjoyment. After all the individual blocks and clones of Pinot Noir — fermented separately — have matured for about 10 months in oak, they are tasted blind, barrel by barrel. The wine from younger vines tends to end up in Crimson.

Ata Rangi describes its 2009 vintage as 'a very serious wine; a broad spread of dark fruits and deep savoury notes, with the classic "peacock's tail" burst of flavour at the end'. After five years or so, the wine becomes very complex, harmonious and 'complete'.

Ata Rangi Pinot Noir enjoys a cult following in New Zealand — and that's one cult I'm happy to belong to.

If you like this wine, also try: Ata Rangi Crimson Pinot Noir; Terravin Hillside Reserve Marlborough Pinot Noir

BANNOCK BRAE
GOLDFIELDS PINOT NOIR

LIKE the goldminers of yore, this tiny Central Otago vineyard has staked out a big claim: 'Bannock Brae Estate is New Zealand's most-awarded single-vineyard Pinot producer. This is based on gold medals won in the four major [annual] New Zealand wine competitions since 2002.'

Owner Crawford Brown and his winemaker Jennifer Parr, of Olssen's Garden Vineyard, get together in December to taste all the barrels, searching for those with the 'seductive, silky texture' that Brown views as the trademark of his wines. Most of the best casks are earmarked for the premium 'Barrel Selection' label, but others are blended with those that miss the cut to create the deliciously perfumed, generous and supple, second-tier label, Goldfields.

Price: **$29**

For a Pinot Noir you can buy for under $30, the Goldfields is surprisingly classy. The 2001, 2002, 2005 and 2006 vintages all collected gold medals at the Air New Zealand Wine Awards.

Crawford and Catherine Brown started planting vines in 1996 on a 'burnt, barren' block at Bannockburn. After 28 years working as a technical brewer for Lion Nathan, Brown is 'comfortable talking about winemaking. Viticulture has been more of a learning curve.'

The grapes are picked in early to mid April, under little or no threat of disease, due to the typically dry weather, 'and hence no horrible sprays'. The vines' yields are very low, and at their very advanced ripeness level of 24 to 25 brix, the grapes are 'sugar-ready' at the same time that stalks, pips and tannins are ripe. 'This gives us the remarkable, silky, velvety mouthfeel so sought after in a premium Pinot Noir.'

Fermentation is encouraged with cultured yeasts and the wine is matured in French oak barrels (26 per cent new in 2008). In favourable vintages, the wine is bottled without fining or filtration.

Brown describes the 2008 as offering 'flavours of cherries, plums and berries. Behind these primary flavours, there is an interesting hint of herbs, mushroom and even liquorice complementing its velvety mouthfeel. All this is integrated with just the right balance of acid and tannins — partly from the grapes themselves, and also judicious use of French oak barrels.'

Akarua, a neighbouring producer, purchased a big slice of the Browns' vineyard in 2010. 'We intend to source fruit from our local region,' says Brown, 'particularly for our Goldfields Pinot, likely to be a blend of home fruit and others'.' On past performance, it'll be a bargain.

BEST BUY

If you like this wine, also try: Bannock Brae Barrel Selection Pinot Noir; Julicher 99 Rows Martinborough Pinot Noir

CARRICK CENTRAL OTAGO PINOT NOIR

MANY wines, revved-up by marketers, scream their merits from the roof-tops, but others succeed in impressing more quietly. Carrick's regional classic definitely falls into the second category.

Top vintages of this Bannockburn label are weighty and densely packed, with rich cherry, plum and spice flavours, complex and savoury, and a firm, sustained finish. A powerful red with impressive stuffing and structure, it's built to last.

Price: $45

The winery, which takes its name from nearby Carrick Range, depicts on its label a knot called the Carrick Bend, chosen to symbolise the 'bringing together of the Central Otago *terroir* and our careful viticultural and winemaking practices'. Steve Green, who founded Carrick in 1994 with his wife, Barbara, 'travels the world on Carrick's behalf, but likes nothing better than to be in a back country hut, enjoying a bottle of Carrick Pinot Noir'. The first wines from their 18-hectare vineyard on north-facing slopes at Cairnmuir flowed in 2000.

The Pinot Noirs have been highly acclaimed. Stephen Tanzer, a top American critic with Burgundy expertise, praised the 2006 vintage: 'Intensely flavoured and serious but at the same time lush and sexy. . . . Distinctly Côte de Nuit-like in style and quality, and very impressive.'

Winemaker Jane Docherty, who has worked in other great Pinot Noir regions like Burgundy and Oregon, joined Carrick in 2008, 'with a hop, skip and a jump down the lake from Felton Road, where she was the assistant winemaker'. The grapes, entirely estate-grown, are harvested by hand during April at 23 to 25 brix; the juice is fermented with natural yeasts; and the wine is matured for a year in French oak barriques (typically 30 per cent new).

Carrick Central Otago Pinot Noir is substantial, concentrated and long-lived. The winery describes its 2009 as revealing 'a complex brooding nose showing layers of black cherry, chocolate and cinnamon. The palate is texturally driven with a richness and density of flavour showing sweet succulent fruit, exotic spice and an aromatic dried herb aspect making for a layered, complex wine. The power and weight are held in check by the fine silky tannins which provide a solid backbone.'

From its oldest vines, Carrick also produces a very bold, generous Excelsior Pinot Noir, barrel-aged for 18 months; and an 'easy-drinking, laidback' Unravelled Pinot Noir, smooth but not simple.

If you like this wine, also try: Carrick Unravelled Central Otago Pinot Noir; Escarpment Vineyard Martinborough Pinot Noir

CHURCH ROAD HAWKE'S BAY MERLOT/ CABERNET SAUVIGNON

≫

IS this New Zealand's best-value red of all? The 2009 vintage now on sale is the twentieth, and every year it's a dark, rich, savoury wine, which would be a good buy at its recommended retail price of $26. At its *real* price in supermarkets, sold mostly on 'promotion' at $15 or less, it offers unbeatable value.

Senior winemaker Chris Scott, who has worked at Church Road — owned by Pernod Ricard NZ — since 1998, says this popular red is 'one of the most challenging and exciting wine styles to produce. There is a synergy between Merlot and Cabernet Sauvignon which, when blended in the right proportions, produces arguably the most complete, complex, fragrant and satisfying style of red wine in the world.'

Price: $15–26

Distinctly Bordeaux-like, Church Road Merlot/ Cabernet Sauvignon offers blackcurrant, plum and spice flavours, showing excellent complexity and density. It shines in blind tastings, despite its low price.

The first vintage flowed in 1990. After acquiring the historic Church Road winery in the late 1980s, Montana (the forerunner of Pernod Ricard NZ) formed a close relationship with Cordier, one of Bordeaux's major wine firms, which gave the company clear guidelines on how to boost its red-wine quality. The wines became riper, richer and rounder, but instead of conforming to the New World, 'fresh and fruity' style, they were more earthy and multi-faceted. 'Some people even complain they are "too French" in style,' says an amused Scott.

The grapes are grown in the Gimblett Gravels, the company-owned Redstone Vineyard in The Triangle, and at Havelock North. The 2009 was blended principally from Merlot (50 per cent) and Cabernet Sauvignon (40 per cent), with a splash of Malbec (8 per cent) and Syrah (2 per cent). Maturation is in French and Hungarian oak barriques (typically 30 per cent new).

Scott sees his 2008 vintage as 'a serious, multidimensional wine in a classic Bordeaux style. . . . A complex array of rich black fruits with subtle spice, sandalwood and violet aromas are complemented by earthy, savoury undertones derived from barrel maturation and a traditional, old-world approach to winemaking. On the palate the wine is rich, yet dry and elegant with a backbone of fine, ripe tannins.'

How does the producer make money when such a consistently rewarding red is sold at such a low price? Don't ask me. Just enjoy the bargain.

If you like this wine, also try: Church Road Reserve Hawke's Bay Merlot/Cabernet Sauvignon; Te Mata Estate Woodthorpe Vineyard Merlot/Cabernet Sauvignon

CLEARVIEW ENIGMA

'WE'VE been making single-vineyard, single-winemaker Merlots for 20 years,' says Hawke's Bay winemaker Tim Turvey. 'Can anyone else claim that for Merlot?'

Turvey established his first vines at Te Awanga in 1988, on a shingly coastal site originally planted by Vidal in 1916. His first Merlot flowed in 1991. From 1994 to 2000 the top Merlot-based red was called Reserve Merlot, but since 2001 it has been labelled Enigma.

Dark, mouthfilling and crammed with ripe-fruit characters, Clearview Enigma is a serious yet sensuous red, with a seductive intensity of spicy, vibrant, almost sweet-tasting flavour.

Price: $45

Turvey, who loves the Merlot-based reds of Pomerol and St Émilion, is after 'French-style complexity, rather than just a straight hit of fruit'. His extremely free-draining estate vineyard consistently produces robust, ripe-tasting, flavour-rich reds.

The quality of the wine reflects several factors, including the maturity of the vines (now up to 23 years old); attention to detail in the vineyard; and the complexity of soil types. The vines are grown directly behind the winery, in a mix of clay and stone. Merlot ripens about 10 days ahead of Cabernet Sauvignon. 'With the sea breezes, we can hold Merlot and hold it, clean as a whistle, until the end of April,' says Turvey. 'We get it really ripe without getting into the rainy season.'

The Merlot grapes are hand-picked at an advanced stage of ripeness (typically 24.5 brix), from vines yielding an average of only 5 to 6 tonnes of grapes per hectare. The wine is matured for the lengthy period of 15 to 18 months in French oak barriques, predominantly new.

Although Merlot-predominant, Enigma includes substantial proportions of other varieties, which Turvey believes adds to its complexity. The 2008 vintage, for instance, is a blend of Merlot (75 per cent), Cabernet Franc (14 per cent) and Malbec (11 per cent). In most years, Cabernet Sauvignon also plays a bit part.

The 1994 and 1996 vintages were both champion Merlot at the Air New Zealand Wine Awards, and the 2006 vintage was champion Merlot at the 2008 New Zealand International Wine Show.

Enigma is a powerful, dark red, fleshy and flavour-packed, in a complex yet upfront style 'which reflects Tim's personality,' laughs his partner, Helma van den Berg. It matures well for five to eight years, unfolding a lovely, fragrant complexity.

If you like this wine, also try: Ngatarawa Alwyn Merlot/Cabernet; Villa Maria Cellar Selection Hawke's Bay Merlot/Cabernet Sauvignon

CLEARVIEW RESERVE CABERNET FRANC

>>>

PERHAPS a Francophile is a red-wine drinker who loves Cabernet Franc! This classic grape of Bordeaux is the foundation of Château Cheval Blanc, the illustrious St Émilion, but lives in the shadow of its frequent partner in blends, the far more widely grown and famous Cabernet Sauvignon — of which it is probably a mutation.

Clearview Estate, a small producer on the Hawke's Bay coastline, has long championed Cabernet Franc. 'If anyone can lay claim to the title of New Zealand's top producer of Cabernet Franc, at this stage the honour belongs to this tiny Te Awanga winery,' I wrote in 1995, shortly after tasting the exceptional 1994 vintage. Since then, little has changed.

Price: $40

Top vintages of Clearview Reserve Cabernet Franc — such as the 2007 and 2009 — are very floral, refined and complex, with deep, blackcurrant-like flavours, hints of nuts, herbs, spices and dark chocolate, and plenty of muscle. A classic claret style, powerful but not heavy, it has a proven ability to flourish for a decade.

Planted most heavily in Hawke's Bay and to a lesser extent Auckland, Cabernet Franc is generally used in New Zealand to add a berryish aroma, fruitiness and genial softness to its blends with Merlot and Cabernet Sauvignon. Tim Turvey, the founder of Clearview Estate, cultivates Cabernet Franc in his shingly estate vineyard, a 'frost-free, amazingly well-drained' site, originally planted by Vidal in 1916.

The grapes are hand-harvested from vines well over 20 years old, with a small portion of younger plantings. Cabernet Franc accounts for 90 per cent of the blend, supplemented by a splash of Merlot and Cabernet Sauvignon, and the wine is matured for 15 months or longer in French oak barriques (mostly new).

A fan of Cabernet Franc, Turvey blends it into several other Clearview Estate reds: Old Olive Block (based on the two Cabernets, supplemented by Merlot and Malbec); Enigma (Merlot-predominant); Two Pinnacles (Malbec-based); and The Basket Press (Cabernet Sauvignon-uppermost).

Enjoyable in its youth, due to its fine, supple tannins, the wine also matures well. Tasted in 2006, the 1998 vintage of Clearview Reserve Cabernet Franc (on sale in the winery restaurant at $120) was rich, cedary and spicy — just like a mature Bordeaux.

CLEARVIEW
ESTATE WINERY

RESERVE CABERNET FRANC
HAWKE'S BAY

13.5% VOL 750ML

PRODUCT OF NEW ZEALAND

If you like this wine, also try: Crossroads Vineyard Selection Mere Road Vineyard Gimblett Gravels Cabernet Franc; Sileni The Pacemaker Hawke's Bay Cabernet Franc

CRAGGY RANGE GIMBLETT GRAVELS VINEYARD MERLOT

DENSELY packed, with a real sense of power and presence, but also more than its fair share of fragrance and finesse, this is a distinguished Hawke's Bay red. At its suggested retail price of $29.95, it must often be underrated.

Like all Craggy Range wines, the Merlot is an expression of a single site. 'The warmth of the vineyard and stony soils help produce very ripe grapes — the essence of our style,' reports the production team, headed by wine and viticulture director Steve Smith, and chief winemaker Rod Easthope. 'Rich, supple black-fruit flavours [with] ample fine-grained tannin, length and lushness.'

Craggy Range's 100-hectare Gimblett Gravels Vineyard, which fans out around the base of Roys Hill, north-west of Hastings, is dedicated principally to the production of claret-style reds, Syrah and Chardonnay. The most extensively planted variety of all is Merlot, but for Bordeaux-style reds the company also established smaller pockets of Cabernet Sauvignon, Malbec, Cabernet Franc and Petit Verdot.

Gimblett Gravels Vineyard Merlot is typically 85 to 88 per cent Merlot, blended with minor portions of Cabernet Franc, Cabernet Sauvignon and Malbec.

Price: $30

The grapes are harvested by hand and machine at an advanced stage of ripeness (typically 23.5 to 24 brix), and the wine is matured for 14 to 18 months in French oak barriques (30 to 45 per cent new).

Craggy Range's winemakers describe the 2009 vintage of this top-value red as exhibiting a 'very dark colour . . . [and] a brooding bouquet of dark plums and blackberry. Wild thyme, rose-like florals and nutmeg nuances contribute to a lifted complexity. The silken texture unveils an intense fruit core with characters of cocoa and fresh tobacco.'

The Gimblett Gravels Vineyard Merlot is consistently a classy, very rich, complex and satisfying wine, as good as — and often superior to — many Hawke's Bay producers' $40 reds.

For Merlot-lovers, Craggy Range produces three other reds well worth discovering. From a subsidiary, Wild Rock Wine Company, comes a bargain-priced Gravel Pit Red Merlot/Malbec, always dark, sturdy and crammed with brambly, spicy flavour. Craggy Range Te Kahu, another great buy, is a mouthfilling, generous and supple blend of Merlot (principally), Cabernet Franc, Cabernet Sauvignon and Malbec. At the top end of the range is Craggy Range Sophia, a highly fragrant, dense and finely textured marriage of 'the very best' Merlot and Cabernet Franc.

BEST BUY

If you like this wine, also try: Alluviale; Clearview Enigma

CRAGGY RANGE LE SOL

ONE of the country's most talked-about wines in recent years, Craggy Range Le Sol ('The Soil') has helped to set a new standard for New Zealand Syrah — intensely varietal, with bottomless depth. A bold, opulent style, it is muscular and densely flavoured, yet also fresh and vibrant, with great power and personality.

Launched from the 2001 vintage, Le Sol swiftly generated international acclaim. Robert Parker, the top American critic, gave the 2002 vintage 94 points out of 100. 'All of Syrah's characteristics — smoke, liquorice, pepper, blackberries and currants — are present in this beautifully knit, pure, concentrated 2002.'

Price: $100

The 2001 to 2004 vintages of Le Sol were made by American Doug Wisor, who was killed in a kite-surfing accident in October 2004. Wisor's key contribution to Le Sol was outlined by Craggy Range in a newsletter shortly before he died. 'In 2001, Craggy was about to harvest its first Syrah in what was a tricky vintage weather-wise. Years of Hawke's Bay experience had Smith [Steve Smith, wine and viticulture director] ready to pull it in before things got worse. Stubbornly, Wisor insisted it hang out longer to be fully ripened. Striking a compromise with his young colleague, Smith brought in the bulk for Block 14 Syrah [now labelled Gimblett Gravels

Vineyard Syrah], leaving the rest until Wisor got the dehydration he sought. The early-picked Syrah equalled most others harvested that year, but the later harvested Le Sol was glorious.'

Le Sol is grown in the company-owned Gimblett Gravels Vineyard. The vines, densely planted in the most gravelly parts of the vineyard, are an old clone of Syrah believed to have been in New Zealand since the early nineteenth century. The grapes are hand-harvested at a 'supremely ripe' stage of maturity, when the berries are soft and slightly dimpled; the juice is fermented with natural yeasts; and the wine is matured for about 20 months in French oak barriques (40 to 50 per cent new).

In the UK, *Decanter* in late 2010 awarded the 2008 vintage 19 out of 20 points: 'Deep, dark, dense and brooding, this is a very rich, complex wine, showing notes of plum, blackberry, aniseed, lavender and vanilla spice. A stunner.'

A majestic wine, Le Sol is all latent power in its youth, suggesting a cellaring potential of 10 to 20 years. This benchmark Hawke's Bay Syrah is one of the most striking of all New Zealand reds.

If you like this wine, also try: Craggy Range Gimblett Gravels Vineyard Syrah; Trinity Hill Homage

DOG POINT VINEYARD MARLBOROUGH PINOT NOIR

GRAPE-grower Ivan Sutherland and winemaker James Healy produced the first Dog Point Vineyard wines in 2004. 'We'd both clocked up 50 years,' recalls Healy. 'So we thought: "Now's the time."'

Sutherland and Healy had for many years been senior members of the Cloudy Bay team, so expectations were high when they set up Dog Point.

Price: $42

Sutherland, from a prominent Marlborough farming family, and his wife, Margaret, own substantial vineyards in the Wairau Valley. Healy, whose wife, Wendy, is a partner in Dog Point Vineyard, has been involved in winemaking since 1979, when he joined Corbans at Henderson, in Auckland, rising to the post of quality control manager.

Dog Point Vineyard — named after a nearby hill, once home to a pack of marauding dogs — lies at the junction of the Brancott and Omaka valleys, on the south side of the Wairau Valley. Sauvignon Blanc is the major variety planted, supplemented by Chardonnay and Pinot Noir.

'We have no desire to be big,' says Margaret Sutherland, 'being totally hands-on, and involved from the vineyard through production to the marketplace.' Dog Point Vineyard is the source of a very elegant, tight, slowly evolving Chardonnay; a funky, minerally and nutty, barrel-aged Sauvignon Blanc, labelled Section 94; and one of Marlborough's most stylish Pinot Noirs.

Healy believes that those who strive to produce great Pinot Noir in Marlborough 'can get the fruit characters and structure they get in Burgundy'. The 2009 Dog Point Vineyard was hand-picked from six Pinot Noir clones, grown in clay soils on slopes and adjacent plots surrounding the winery. The vines were cropped extremely lightly (5 tonnes of grapes per hectare).

At the winery, after hand-sorting to remove inferior bunches and berries, the grapes are de-stemmed and transferred to open-topped tanks, where the juice ferments with natural yeasts. After it has been pressed from the skins, the wine matures for 18 months in French oak barrels (typically 50 per cent new) and is then bottled without fining or filtering.

Top vintages of Dog Point Vineyard Pinot Noir are a lovely mouthful. A graceful, full-bodied and supple red, with sweet-fruit delights, it offers cherry, plum, spice and nut flavours that build across the palate to a rich, rounded finish.

A wine of great finesse, it's a 'feminine' style of Pinot Noir, beautifully flowing and floral.

If you like this wine, also try: Fromm Clayvin Vineyard Marlborough Pinot Noir; Villa Maria Cellar Selection Marlborough Pinot Noir

ESCARPMENT MARTINBOROUGH PINOT NOIR

>>> ANYONE can grow it,' Larry McKenna told Dave Cull in *A Toast to Martinborough and the Wairarapa* (2003). 'Anyone can make it [Pinot Noir]. . . . But turning it into money: that's the trick. It made life easier knowing we had some sort of brand, some sort of position. The brand was McKenna, Pinot Noir and Martinborough.'

Price: $45

- - - - - - - - - - - - - - - - - - - -

For many wine lovers, Larry McKenna's name is inextricably linked with Martinborough Vineyard, where he produced a pioneering series of top-flight Pinot Noirs between 1986 and 1999. In his later years, as the company's winemaker and general manager — which got him travelling the world to promote the wine — McKenna was *the* public face of Martinborough wine.

Today, at Escarpment Vineyard, owned by McKenna and his wife, Sue, and Australians Robert and Mem Kirby, he makes six Pinot Noirs. Apart from The Edge Martinborough Pinot Noir, a good-value, drink-young style, Escarpment also produces a flagship, dark and dense Pinot Noir, labelled as Kupe, and a trio of single-vineyard Pinot Noirs. This middle-tier wine is the key label.

Seductively perfumed, with rich flavours of plums,

spices, herbs and nuts, it is typically a complex red, very savoury and harmonious. It offers good cellaring potential, but is also delicious in its youth.

Site selection is the critical factor if you want to produce great Pinot Noir, McKenna told *New Zealand Winegrower*. 'That is most important, and you must match everything about the planting, clones, rootstock, spacing and trellis to it. If the site is ideal and harmonised to the viticulture, then — depending on the weather — the fruit can be of exceptional quality, which makes winemaking a piece of cake.'

Although principally estate-grown at Te Muna, a few kilometres south-east of the township, Escarpment Martinborough Pinot Noir is a district blend made from hand-picked grapes, handled very gently in the winery until pressed. During the fermentation, the skins are hand-plunged into the juice every eight hours, and the wine is matured for nearly a year in French oak barriques (30 per cent new).

What is the Escarpment style? McKenna sees it as 'complexity, attractive texture and the perfect mix of black, red and green fruit flavours for which Pinot Noir is celebrated'. The hallmarks of his 2009 vintage, he says, are 'perfume, elegant fruit flavours and soft, ripe tannins'.

Twenty-five years ago, McKenna was the first experienced winemaker to arrive in Martinborough. You can taste that in this superbly supple, savoury and scented red.

If you like this wine, also try: The Edge Martinborough Pinot Noir; Carrick Central Otago Pinot Noir

ESK VALLEY THE TERRACES

>>>

SOLD *en primeur* for $99 and on the shelves at around $125, The Terraces is one of New Zealand's most expensive reds — but also one of the greatest, with enormous scale and bottomless depth. An excitingly bold, dark Hawke's Bay wine with intense, plummy, spicy, complex flavours, braced by firm tannins, it rewards cellaring for up to a decade — even beyond.

Soon after Villa Maria purchased the Esk Valley winery (then called Glenvale) in 1987, a steep, terraced hillside bordering the winery at Bay View, originally planted with vines in the 1940s but later established in pines, was replanted in Merlot, Malbec, Cabernet Sauvignon and Cabernet Franc. Today, this densely planted, drought-prone, irrigated vineyard each year yields an exceptional red wine — The Terraces. 'I'm the custodian of one of New Zealand's greatest vineyards,' says winemaker Gordon Russell.

Price: **$100–130**

The land faces north to north-west, giving the vines long exposure to sunshine. The soils, uplifted over millions of years, are a complex mix of layers of shells, limestone, lumps of clay and river shingle. It is a free-draining, frost-free site, and although close to the ocean, sheltered from sea breezes.

The vines, although mostly 22 years old (the area devoted to Malbec was extended in

1996) are still small: 'They've had to struggle to survive,' says Russell. It's an unusually hot, very early-ripening site, and the vines' yields are very low, averaging only 5 tonnes per hectare.

The Terraces is a triumphant expression of site selection and vine management, rather than vinification. 'At the winery, it's very hands-off. All three of the grape varieties go into a single, open-topped fermenter, so that removes blending options, allowing the vineyard and nature to truly create the wine.' Maturation is for up to 22 months in all-new French oak barriques.

Muscular, with a scale, warmth and flavour depth rare in New Zealand reds, The Terraces is a dark, spicy, meaty, tannic red, with a distinctive extra dimension that reflects its high Malbec content. Malbec accounts for 43 per cent of the vines, followed by Merlot (35 per cent) and Cabernet Franc (22 per cent); the Malbec, says Russell, gives 'perfume, spice, tannin and brilliant colour'.

The wine is not entered in competitions. 'It's not a show wine,' says Russell. 'It is the most expensive wine made by the Villa Maria group — a symbol of what we can do.'

If you like this wine, also try: Stonyridge Luna Negra Malbec; Esk Valley Winemakers Reserve Merlot/Cabernet Sauvignon/Malbec

ESK VALLEY WINEMAKERS RESERVE GIMBLETT GRAVELS MERLOT/CABERNET SAUVIGNON/MALBEC

≫

THIS voluptuous red is one of New Zealand's most acclaimed Merlot-based wines, with a host of major awards to its credit. Its exact name has varied over the years, but the wine is always dark, richly perfumed and lush, with intense, plummy, sweet-fruit flavours that give it great drink-young appeal, but also the power and structure to mature well for several years.

Price: **$60**

Why is it a blend of three Bordeaux varieties, rather than a straight varietal Merlot? 'We start with a Merlot base [over 50 per cent of the final blend] and work outwards,' says winemaker Gordon Russell. 'Merlot provides the heart — a gobful of plums and fruit cake. We add Malbec for colour, spice and front-palate sweetness, and Cabernet Sauvignon for tannin and structure. Each vintage, we build the best wine, given that year's resources.'

The Esk Valley winery, on the coast at Bay View, is owned by Villa Maria, and Russell attributes the quality of the Winemakers Reserve red to the group's extensive vineyard resources. Since 1995, the grapes have come almost exclusively 'off the stones' — the company-owned Ngakirikiri Vineyard, near Gimblett Road, and the neighbouring Cornerstone Vineyard.

In warm, dry shingle country the fruit ripens earlier, says Russell, 'with riper flavours and greater elegance and perfume'.

In their pursuit of a 'mouth-watering, not mouth-puckering' style of Merlot, Esk Valley's winemakers ferment the wine in 75-year-old, open-topped concrete vats and plunge the grapes' skins into the juice by hand. The wine is matured for about 20 months in French oak barriques (60 to 80 per cent new).

Esk Valley's reserve Merlot-based red has performed brilliantly on the show circuit for many years; the 1990 vintage was the overall champion wine of the 1991 Air New Zealand Wine Awards. More recently, the 2007 vintage won a gold medal at the Liquorland Top 100 International Wine Competition in 2009.

Dark, vibrantly fruity and bursting with ripe, sweet-tasting blackcurrant, plum and French oak flavours, this is one of the country's classiest claret-style reds. I like it at three to five years old, when it is still exuberantly fresh and fruity.

If you like this wine, also try: Clearview Enigma; Villa Maria Cellar Selection Hawke's Bay Merlot/Cabernet Sauvignon

FELTON ROAD BANNOCKBURN CENTRAL OTAGO PINOT NOIR

TWENTY years ago, the land beneath Felton Road's estate vineyard, The Elms, was a bare Bannockburn valley, overlooked by wine-growers and untouched by gold miners. Today, Felton Road enjoys a worldwide reputation for its gloriously scented, savoury and seamless Pinot Noirs.

Price: $49

Right from the start, the wine has stirred up excitement; the debut 1997 vintage sold for US$45 in the United States. 'Every wine region needs a hero,' according to *Decanter* magazine, in the UK. 'Sauternes has Yquem, Central Otago has Felton Road.'

This is the winery's large-volume wine, in the past called Central Otago Pinot Noir, but since 2009 also labelled boldly as Bannockburn. Although not Felton Road's greatest red, it is a distinguished wine in its own right, typically very graceful and generous, showing lovely richness and harmony.

Felton Road farms three properties, totalling 32 hectares, at Bannockburn: The Elms, Cornish Point and Calvert. This wine is a blend of grapes from the three sites. But the winery also produces single-vineyard Pinot Noirs from Cornish Point and Calvert, and Block 3 and Block 5 Pinot Noirs from The Elms.

Does this weaken the larger-volume blend?

'We don't see this as a problem at all,' Felton Road declared in 2008. 'Firstly, vine age is starting to really play a more important factor in this blend. The oldest vines at Elms vineyard are now 16 years old and the youngest vines going into the blend are 6 years old. . . . The single vineyard wines are not selected on size or impact, but on their ability to express the personality of the site. Sometimes . . . the vineyard-designated wines can be quite a bit lighter in weight than the Felton Road Pinot Noir.'

A fully organic and biodynamic producer (certified by Demeter), Felton Road adopts a 'hands-off' approach in the winery, to 'preserve the wine's expression of its *terroir*'. The 2009 vintage was fermented with natural yeasts, matured for 11 months in French oak barrels, and bottled without fining or filtering.

Felton Road describes the 2009 vintage as revealing a 'spicier' perfume, 'with chocolate and violets overlaying dark cherry and raspberry. The palate is seamlessly plush and richly textural, with significant, very fine, dusty tannins.' Floral and supple, yet also savoury and dense, it's a classic Felton Road.

If you like this wine, also try: Felton Road Block 5 Pinot Noir; Peregrine Central Otago Pinot Noir 〈〈〈

FROMM CLAYVIN VINEYARD PINOT NOIR

PINOT Noir accounts for more than half of this small, Swiss-owned Marlborough winery's output. 'We want long-lived wine, with tannin structure and generosity,' says Hätsch Kalberer, winemaker since the first 1992 vintage.

Clayvin Vineyard is Fromm's 'most opulent and seductive Pinot Noir'. Deeply coloured, it is fragrant and supple, with deep plum, spice and nut flavours, complex, finely poised and rich. It's an authoritative red, but highly approachable.

Fromm produces two single-vineyard Pinot Noirs. Those from Clayvin Vineyard are rich, elegant and relatively accessible in their youth. By contrast, those from the more gravelly Fromm Vineyard, on the floor of the Wairau Valley, are more masculine, densely packed and firm.

Price: **$60**

Georg Fromm, the founder of Fromm Winery, is no longer involved, but still grows and makes Pinot Noir in Switzerland. Single-vineyard Pinot Noirs, he believes, are 'all about expressing the vineyard character, site, soil and micro-climate. The sensitive and fragile yet complex nature of the Pinot Noir grape, known for its ability to mutate and adjust to its environment, is capable of producing the most exciting expressions of *terroir*.'

The 15-hectare Clayvin Vineyard lies on north-facing slopes in the Brancott Valley. The clay soil, from which the vineyard takes its name, gives the red wines 'richness and generosity and an immediately appealing soft texture'.

Kalberer is not one of those winemakers who believe grapes grow on the back of trucks. 'Our philosophy places *terroir* over technology, and grape quality over quantity.' To create wines capable of offering pleasure over many years, Kalberer and William Hoare, his co-winemaker, reduce the vines' yields to 5 tonnes of fruit per hectare.

The grapes are picked by hand and the juice is fermented with natural yeasts. The wine is matured in 228-litre *pieces* (Burgundy barrels), with only 10 to 15 per cent new wood each year.

Fromm describes the 2007 as having a classic Clayvin bouquet, with 'dark chocolate and earthy, red cherry aromas. The palate is savoury and complex with beautifully integrated tannins, giving this otherwise softly textured wine the necessary spine and structure for aging.'

Fromm doesn't participate in competitions. Occasionally, overseas, others have entered its wines in comparative judgings — and its drink-young, La Strada red has performed best. 'This reinforces what we always believed, that it lies in the nature of the finest, age-worthy wines not to attract the most attention in commercially orientated tastings.'

If you like this wine, also try: Fromm Fromm Vineyard Pinot Noir; Terravin Hillside Reserve Marlborough Pinot Noir

GIBBSTON VALLEY RESERVE PINOT NOIR

WHEN Central Otago started to rival Martinborough in the mid to late 1990s for the title of New Zealand's top Pinot Noir region, the challenge was initially based on the glittering show success of Gibbston Valley Reserve Pinot Noir.

The 1996 vintage was judged overall champion of the 1998 Liquorland Royal Easter Wine Show — the first time either a Pinot Noir or a Central Otago wine had topped the judging. Grant Taylor, then winemaker at Gibbston Valley, recalls: 'The trophy was a very big cup and during a vaguely remembered night of celebration, almost every bar in Queenstown filled it for us with Speight's.'

Price: $100

The 2000 vintage took a big step further, winning the trophy for champion Pinot Noir at the 2001 International Wine Challenge in London. Two years ago, a British honeymoon couple from Hong Kong paid $1000 for the wine at Gantley's restaurant, near Queenstown.

Over the years, the fruit has been drawn from various sites and sub-regions. The 1995 to 1998 vintages were based mostly on grapes grown in the relatively warm Cromwell Basin, but later Wanaka and Gibbston grapes became more prominent. The 2008 — the first vintage to be a single-vineyard wine — was grown in the company's School House vineyard at Bendigo.

Labelled as 'the pinnacle of our winegrowing',

the Reserve Pinot Noir is designed for up to 10 years' cellaring. Top vintages are perfumed, lush and exuberantly fruity, in a very powerful, flavour-crammed style. The latest releases are the best: finely textured, superbly rich and harmonious.

Gibbston Valley Reserve Pinot Noir 2008 won a gold medal and the trophy for champion Pinot Noir at the 2010 Sydney International Wine Competition. The winery describes it as possessing 'a strikingly floral nose, with ripe plum and cinnamon undertones. A beautiful Pinot impression is created that beguiles, and eschews the obvious. On the palate, the majesty of the wine unfolds. Sublimely silky and initially expansive, a tryst of minerality and tannin work and fuse in with the fruit. . . . Very fine and long.'

If $100 is beyond your budget, Gibbston Valley produces several excellent reds. One of my favourites is the classy Gibbston Valley Central Otago Pinot Noir, less than half the price of the Reserve, but still deliciously fragrant and flavour-packed.

If you like this wine, also try: Gibbston Valley Central Otago Pinot Noir; Ata Rangi Martinborough Pinot Noir

HANS HERZOG MARLBOROUGH MONTEPULCIANO

A colossus of a red, in top vintages this wine overflows with flavour — blackcurrant, plum, spice, liquorice and coffee. Opaque and robust, it's based on a variety as famous in Italy as it is obscure in New Zealand vineyards.

Across central-eastern Italy, Montepulciano yields fleshy, rich reds. A key expression is Montepulciano d'Abruzzo — easy to find on shelves here — and Montepulciano is also the foundation of noble Rosso Conero, grown on the Adriatic coast.

Price: $64

Hans and Therese Herzog, who planted their first vines in Marlborough in 1996, once ran a top Pinot Noir-producing vineyard and restaurant in Switzerland. At Rapaura, on the north side of the Wairau Valley, they grow a broad selection of varieties, including two classic grapes of Italy, Nebbiolo and Montepulciano. Their vines are cropped extremely lightly (below 5 tonnes of grapes per hectare).

Right from the start, Montepulciano shone. *Decanter*, in the UK, gave the 2001 vintage five stars. 'Hans Herzog is not the first New Zealand winemaker to make Montepulciano but he has certainly produced the best — it stands head and shoulders above the others. This dense and savoury red promises to cellar for at least eight years.'

Even the Australians — no strangers to bold reds — rave about it. 'Not only is the '02 exceptionally rare, it is a brilliant wine,' enthused Huon Hooke in the *Sydney Morning Herald*. 'It's a wonderfully rich and eerily Italianate red, scented with dried herbs and flowers, earthy aromas and a hint of bitter cherry that takes you all the way to the Abruzzi.'

The grapes are harvested by hand with high sugar levels (around 25 brix) and the juice is fermented with natural yeasts. After maturing for two years in French oak casks (partly new), the wine is bottled unfined and unfiltered, with moderate acidity and a high level of alcohol (typically 14.5 per cent or more).

Hans describes his Montepulciano as 'a full-bodied and deep, dark cherry-coloured wine, bursting with power'. The bouquet is 'heady', with 'cranberry and dark, ripe plums, underpinned by liquorice and savoury overtones. A voluptuous wine which will age gracefully over the next decade.'

Herzog also makes a rare grappa (grape-based brandy) from Montepulciano . . . but that's another story. Don't miss the arrestingly rich red.

If you like this wine, also try: Black Barn Hawke's Bay Montepulciano; Weeping Sands Waiheke Island Montepulciano

JULICHER 99 ROWS MARTINBOROUGH PINOT NOIR

MANY wine lovers first heard of Julicher (pronounced 'U-li-ker') when its flagship 2008 Martinborough Pinot Noir won the trophy for overall champion of the 2009 Air New Zealand Wine Awards. But the '99 Rows' Pinot Noir is significantly cheaper and amazingly good for a second-tier label.

Take the 2009 vintage. Robust and full-coloured, it is very generous, warm and savoury, with ripe, supple tannins and excellent flavour richness and complexity. During 2010, it scooped gold medals at the New Zealand International Wine Show and the Hong Kong International Wine Show. That's no fluke. Both the 2006 and 2008 vintages of 99 Rows collected gold medals at the Air New Zealand Wine Awards. Widely available at $29.95, it's a consistently delicious, great-value red.

Price: $30

Wilhelmus ('Wim') Julicher arrived in New Zealand from the Netherlands in 1972. After an abortive attempt in the late 1990s to establish a large olive grove and tiny vineyard at Martinborough, he changed direction and today has a small olive grove and large, 20-hectare vineyard.

Julicher Estate's vineyard and winery lie in Te Muna Road, a few kilometres south-east of

Martinborough township. In free-draining alluvial soils, the first variety planted was Pinot Noir. Outi Jakovirta, the Finnish winemaker, has worked in Europe, the US, Australia and at Martinborough Vineyard.

99 Rows Pinot Noir is made entirely from estate-grown grapes, harvested by hand from various clones and blocks at an advanced stage of ripeness (23 to 25 brix). The juice is fermented with cultured yeasts and the wine ages for 10 months in French oak barrels. New oak has a declining role. The 2004 vintage was matured in all-new casks, but in 2006, 50 per cent of the casks were new. Today, about 15 to 20 per cent of the barrels used for 99 Rows are new, which allows the wine's seductively rich and ripe fruit characters to shine through in its youth.

Julicher describes 99 Rows as having an aroma of 'raspberries, ripe cherries and wild strawberries with a soft, savoury and spicy complexity'. On the palate, it is 'medium-bodied and balanced with soft tannins and bright red fruit carrying through onto a long finish'.

A lovely combination of charm and complexity, 99 Rows is an intensely varietal wine, cherryish, spicy, rich and supple. For a sub-$30 Pinot Noir, it's hard to beat.

BEST BUY

If you like this wine, also try: Julicher Martinborough Pinot Noir; Bannock Brae Goldfields Central Otago Pinot Noir

KENNEDY POINT WAIHEKE ISLAND SYRAH

KENNEDY Points to Red Heaven' trumpeted a 2009 headline in the *Sunday Star-Times*. The paper was celebrating the success of Kennedy Point Waiheke Island Syrah 2007, which had just scooped a gold medal and the trophies for Best New Zealand Red and Best International Syrah at one of the world's biggest wine competitions, the London-based International Wine Challenge.

Price: **$45**

Set amid old pohutukawa at the western entrance to Putiki Bay, on the south-west side of the island, Kennedy Point Vineyard was founded by Susan McCarthy and Neal Kunimura in 1996. The couple came to Waiheke from another island — Oahu, the third-largest of the Hawaiian Islands. Kunimura runs the grapegrowing side of the venture, while McCarthy oversees the marketing.

The estate vineyard, adjacent to the winery and cellar door, has 2 hectares of Cabernet Sauvignon and Syrah planted in north-facing clay soils. Kennedy Point also draws Syrah grapes from two other sites: Oakura Bay Vineyard, near Te Whau winery, on the far side of the bay from Kennedy Point; and Jasa Vineyard, at the head of Putiki Bay, established in 2001 solely in Syrah.

At first, Kennedy Point was best known for sturdy, savoury, Bordeaux-style reds, based on Cabernet Sauvignon, Merlot and Malbec. However, Syrah has now stepped boldly into the limelight.

Herb Friedli, a Swiss who has lived on Waiheke since 1994, makes the wine for several of the island's producers, including Kennedy Point. The internationally acclaimed Syrah is co-fermented with 2 per cent Viognier, to enhance its perfume and fruitiness, and matured for 19 months in French oak casks.

Decanter, the influential UK wine magazine, also raved about Kennedy Point Syrah 2007. 'Expressive Syrah, showcasing the potential of the grape in New Zealand. Dark and peppery, it's laden with highly scented, purply fruit that provide a fine counterpoint to the inky core. The flavours fill the mouth and really grab your attention. Great stuff.'

The 2008 vintage is equally memorable. Powerful, yet elegant and supple, it's a finely perfumed, dark red with a lovely array of blackcurrant, plum, spice, liquorice and nut flavours, rich and rounded. The 2006, tasted in 2009, was maturing superbly.

This rare, distinctly classy wine is well worth tracking down.

If you like this wine, also try: Passage Rock Reserve Syrah; Mills Reef Elspeth Syrah

KIDNAPPER CLIFFS HAWKE'S BAY PINOTAGE

WHEN I tasted the debut 2009 vintage of this Gimblett Gravels red, I pondered whether it was New Zealand's best-ever Pinotage. From Te Awa, a winery with a strong reputation for Pinotage, it is exceptionally concentrated, vibrant and supple, with none of the rusticity which can plague this variety.

Bob Campbell, a New Zealand wine writer and Master of Wine, also praised

Price: $45

it, giving it 93 points out of 100. 'Ripe plum, spice and classy oak are the most obvious flavours but they are supported by many more subtle nuances. Beautifully structured red with good development potential.' In a blind tasting, Campbell said he would pick the wine as 'a robust Pinot Noir', while I wrote it 'could easily be mistaken for Syrah', but he agreed it was 'quite possibly the best Pinotage ever made in New Zealand'.

Pinotage has a humble image in New Zealand. A South African cross of the classic Pinot Noir variety of Burgundy with the heavier-yielding Cinsaut grape, grown widely across the south of France, it is favoured for its good disease-resistance and ability to produce large volumes of berryish, spicy wine, typically best enjoyed young.

Te Awa, founded in the early 1990s, is known

for savoury, Merlot-based, Bordeaux-style reds. Te Awa has also long produced one of New Zealand's greatest Pinotages — arguably *the* greatest — densely coloured, robust, brambly and spicy.

The 17-hectare Kidnapper Cliffs vineyard has been 'parcelled out from Te Awa's mature vineyard holdings [50 hectares] specifically for its relatively uniform, free-draining soil and consistent production of high quality fruit'. The goal is to create 'low-yield, niche wines structured for long-term cellaring'.

Winemaker Ant Mackenzie, who joined Te Awa in 2009, is a Hawke's Bay local who in the past produced top wines at Spy Valley, and earlier Framingham, in Marlborough. 'Our sense is that many untried varieties have tremendous potential in this prime vineyard.' His 2009 Pinotage, Mackenzie says, has 'a nose which speaks of an armful of roses, red-skinned apples and baking spice. Layers of fine fruit tannin and savoury characters balance the flamboyant berry fruit and rose petal flavours.'

Kidnapper Cliffs has set out 'to explore the full potential of this somewhat unfashionable variety,' Mackenzie reports. With their unprecedentedly classy 2009 Pinotage, they are off to a great start.

WINE OF NEW ZEALAND

KIDNAPPER CLIFFS
PINOTAGE
2009
Hawkes Bay

If you like this wine, also try: Muddy Water Waipara Pinotage; Karikari Estate Pinotage

LA COLLINA SYRAH

≫

ITALIAN for 'the hill', la collina (pronounced *col-ee-na*) is a brand of Bilancia, a small wine company in Hawke's Bay. The Syrah is typically a majestic red, one of the greatest in the country.

Dark, savoury, complex and dense, la collina (as it is usually called) is an arresting wine, highly concentrated and built for the long haul. Part-owner and senior national wine judge Warren Gibson told *New Zealand Grapegrower* that he buys and drinks Syrah 'more often than any other variety. It is what keeps me in Hawke's Bay from a New Zealand winemaking perspective.'

Price: $90

Gibson — who in 2010 was appointed executive winemaker at Trinity Hill — and his partner, Lorraine Leheny, say Bilancia is Italian for 'balance' or 'harmony', qualities the couple aspire to achieve in their wines. Since 1998, the northern slopes of 'la collina', their steep, terraced vineyard on Roys Hill, overlooking the Gimblett Gravels, have been planted solely in Syrah. Viognier is cultivated at the base.

Hand-picked during April with up to three 'passes' through the vineyard, the grapes are co-fermented with a splash of Viognier (about 2 per cent) and the wine is matured for 20 months or so in French oak casks. 'The wine seems to prefer little intervention whilst it is resting in barrel,' Gibson and Leheny find. 'The winemaking philosophy has always been to preserve the very distinct vineyard character and fruit purity along with support from new, but low-impact, French oak.'

In the US, the *Wine Advocate* gave the 2004 vintage 93 points/100; the 2005 91; the 2006 93. *Decanter*, in the UK, declared in 2008: 'Although it is way too premature to suggest that Hawke's Bay Syrah is giving the Northern Rhône the same kind of headache as Sauvignon Blanc did to Baron de Ladoucette, I imagine that if the two Bilancia wines were served blind to Marcel Guigal, the Rhône stalwart would be suitably impressed. Perhaps he may even raise his trademark beret in salute.'

Apart from its great, strikingly deep, multi-faceted la collina red, Bilancia also produces an excellent, much lower-priced Syrah/Viognier, sourced partly from la collina; and since 2008 a weighty, ripe and rounded, peach and spice-flavoured 'la collina White', blended from Viognier (mostly) and Gewürztraminer.

If you like this wine, also try: Bilancia Syrah/Viognier; Trinity Hill Homage Syrah

MARTINBOROUGH VINEYARD PINOT NOIR

THIS was New Zealand's first consistently classy Pinot Noir. From vines up to 30 years old, it is instantly likeable, but also shows real density and maturation potential. In top vintages it is deeply coloured and finely perfumed, with concentrated, beautifully ripe plum, cherry and spice flavours, complex, savoury and supple.

The superb 1986 vintage was the first to transcend the simple, shallow style of Pinot Noir that was previously the norm here. Early vintages won the trophy for champion Pinot Noir at the Air New Zealand Wine Awards in 1988, 1989 and 1990, giving the wine an illustrious reputation that it retains today.

Price: $70

Duncan Milne, who with his brother Derek is one of the founders of Martinborough Vineyard, recalls the partners' first meeting. 'Derek brought along a bottle of *grand cru* Burgundy, popped it on the table, pulled the cork, and said: "This is the objective."'

Larry McKenna (now at Escarpment) was the winemaker from 1986 to 1999, followed by Claire Mulholland. Since 2007, the wines have been made by Paul Mason, who has worked in several overseas regions, including Burgundy. Mason believes the company's oldest vines on the Martinborough Terrace are 'now beginning to show a real sense of place or *terroir*. This is most evident on the palate where the older vines produce a wine showing greater complexity and depth.'

The grapes are hand-picked at 23 to 25.5 brix. The fruit is carefully sorted in the vineyard and again at the winery, before being transferred to small, open-top fermenting vats. The juice is fermented with natural yeasts and the wine, matured for a year in French oak barriques (33 per cent new), is bottled without fining or filtering.

Mason describes the 2008 vintage as offering a bouquet of 'black cherry, dark chocolate and Asian spice notes that will typically change to savoury, earthy characters as the wine ages. On the palate the layers of dark fruits are beautifully entwined with soft, velvety tannins and a seamless texture. This wine exhibits power and poise and will age gracefully for 10+ years.'

The flow of awards, so striking in the early years, hasn't dried up — the 2004, 2005, 2006 and 2007 vintages of Martinborough Vineyard Pinot Noir all collected gold medals in London. Martinborough Vineyard also produces several other reds, notably a hedonistic, rare, barrel-selected Marie Zelie Reserve Pinot Noir and a fleshy and savoury, sharply priced Te Tera Pinot Noir.

If you like this wine, also try: Martinborough Vineyard Te Tera Pinot Noir; Ata Rangi Pinot Noir

MILLS REEF
ELSPETH SYRAH

THIS is a star Syrah. Since the debut 1998 vintage, most releases have won a gold medal and some have won several, in New Zealand, Australia and the UK. The 2007 vintage, for instance, collected several five-star awards, an elite gold medal at the 2009 Air New Zealand Wine Awards, and a Top 100 blue-gold medal at the 2010 Sydney International Wine Competition.

Overflowing with blackcurrant/spice flavours, Mills Reef Elspeth Syrah offers precisely defined varietal characters, coupled with the warmth and generosity of top Hawke's Bay reds. 'Our goals are to express the site and variety,' says Tim Preston, a son of the founders, Paddy and Helen Preston. 'We also aim to add complexity in the winery and produce a style that is Syrah [modelled on France's Rhône Valley] rather than Shiraz [Australia].'

Price: $40

The grapes are usually — but not always — sourced solely from the company's shingly, silty, free-draining property in Mere Road, planted in 1993 near Stonecroft winery, the pioneer of outstanding Syrah in New Zealand. 'It's one of the best sites in the Gimblett Gravels,' says Preston. 'You can see that late in the season, when other vines are closing down, but those in the Elspeth block are still in good health.'

The grapes are harvested by hand when very ripe (around 24 brix) and the juice is fermented with natural yeasts in 400-litre French *intégrale* barrels, rotated twice daily. By slowly rotating the juice through the skins, rather than punching the 'cap' of skins into the fermenting juice, the Prestons feel they achieve more refined, supple tannins in the wine, which is then matured for up to 16 months in French oak barriques (80 per cent new in 2006; 65 per cent new in 2007).

Mills Reef describes the 2007 vintage as a 'generous, fragrant red' with 'luscious, multi-faceted aromas of ripe blackcurrant, blueberry and ground pepper, with layers of caramel, chocolate, smoke, spice, nutmeg and cloves. The palate is rich and weighty, yet smooth and supple, with fine tannins and classic varietal flavours — brambly blackcurrant, dark chocolate, spice and white pepper.'

If you are a fan of Syrah, Mills Reef also has an excellent, fine-value Reserve Hawke's Bay Syrah, made with some use of Viognier and American oak; and a distinguished Elspeth Trust Vineyard Syrah.

If you like this wine, also try: Mills Reef Reserve Hawke's Bay Syrah; Passage Rock Reserve Syrah

MUDDY WATER
SLOWHAND PINOT NOIR

≫ 'FROM our oldest vines, this single-vineyard wine is absolutely out of this world.' That's how Muddy Water promoted the 2009 Slowhand Pinot Noir on its website.

Over the top? At the time of writing, I hadn't tasted the 2009, but given the compelling nature of past vintages, the claim didn't seem outrageous.

Based on the oldest vines, 'tended by slow hands', Muddy Water Slowhand Pinot Noir has revealed an outstanding personality. Dense, savoury and silky, it's an exciting mouthful.

Price: $75

Waipara means 'Muddy Water'. Michael East, a Christchurch obstetrician and gynaecologist, and his wife, Jane, who has a postgraduate diploma in viticulture and oenology, established their first vines in limestone-rich soils at Waipara in 1993. The 18-hectare Muddy Water vineyard, planted principally in Pinot Noir, achieved organic certification in late 2010.

Launched from the 2000 vintage — and at first called Mojo — Slowhand is hand-harvested at an advanced stage of ripeness (24 to 25.5 brix) from ultra low-yielding vines (just 2.2 tonnes of grapes per hectare in 2007; 4 tonnes of grapes per hectare in 2009). The vines are all of the AM10/5 clone, one of the first commercially available Pinot Noir clones in New Zealand. Fermented with natural yeasts, Slowhand Pinot Noir is matured for 15 months in

French oak barrels (30 per cent new) and bottled unfiltered.

Full-bodied, concentrated and soft, notably complex and savoury, Slowhand is a magical red, the sort that lingers in your mind long after the last glass has evaporated. Muddy Water also produces other impressive Pinot Noirs, including Hare's Breath, from a block on limestone soils at the rear of the property that has been home 'to a particularly large hare'.

In March 2011, Jane East announced the sale of Muddy Water to the adjacent Greystone Wines. Belinda Gould, Muddy Water's highly acclaimed winemaker since 2000, is no longer involved, but the Greystone team, says East, will 'keep the brand and continue with its organic production'.

If you like this wine, also try: Muddy Water Waipara Pinot Noir; Terravin Hillside Reserve Marlborough Pinot Noir

NGATARAWA ALWYN MERLOT/CABERNET

THE princely sum of nearly $10,000 was paid in March 2011 for a magnum (1.5 L bottle) of the 2000 vintage of Ngatarawa's flagship red, Alwyn Merlot/Cabernet. The rare wine, released in 2002 to celebrate the Corban family's centenary of winemaking in New Zealand, was auctioned by the Chinese community in Auckland to raise funds for the Christchurch earthquake relief fund.

After 30 years of making wine in Hawke's Bay, Alwyn Corban says the Alwyn selection (which also features a Chardonnay and Noble Harvest Riesling) represents 'the finest wines Ngatarawa produces. . . . I am proud they carry my name, signature and thumb print.'

Price: $55

The first Alwyn Merlot/Cabernet flowed in 1998. Top vintages are majestic reds, dark and plump, rich and savoury, with lots of coffee and spice complexity. Highly concentrated, with sweet-fruit delights and buried tannins, they have the power and structure to flourish for a decade.

For Corban, the wine is all about the fruit it is made from. Alwyn reds 'are an expression of the vineyards where they are grown . . . the wines rely heavily on fruit ripeness and concentration (through low yields) to provide the flavour, body and texture of the wine in the bottle'.

The grapes are grown at two sites — one in The

Triangle, where the Ngatarawa winery is based; the other in the Gimblett Gravels — identified for their consistently outstanding performance over many years. The fruit is harvested by hand from low-yielding vines (typically only 6 tonnes per hectare) and the wine is matured for a year to 16 months in French oak barriques (37 per cent new in 2009).

Merlot dominates, but Cabernet Sauvignon makes a significant contribution, accounting for 20 to 25 per cent of the blend. Corban describes his flagship red as having a bouquet of 'blackberry and black doris plums with integrated charry oak'. On the palate, it is 'rich and concentrated [with] dark plum, cigar box and berries [and] a long, sweet, fruit-cake and spice finish'.

The 2007 vintage of Alwyn Merlot/Cabernet won a gold medal at the 2010 *Decanter* World Wine Awards. Corban and winemaker Peter Gough, who has worked at Ngatarawa since 1993, also produce several other good, lower-priced Merlots under the Ngatarawa Stables, Ngatarawa Stables Reserve, Ngatarawa Silks and Glazebrook Regional Reserve labels.

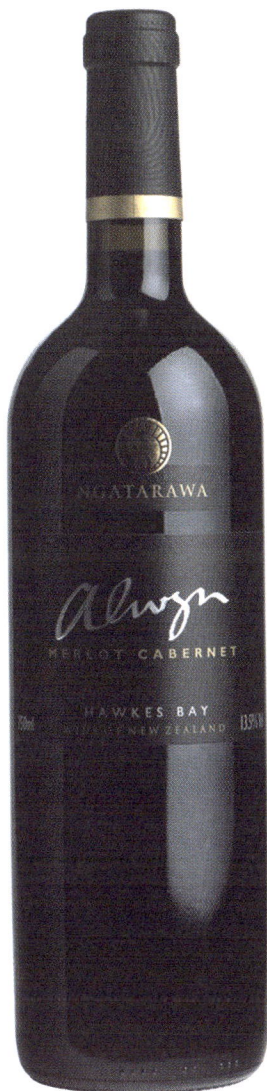

If you like this wine, also try: Puriri Hills Reserve; Church Road Reserve Hawke's Bay Merlot/Cabernet Sauvignon

PASSAGE ROCK RESERVE SYRAH

>>> THIS small producer claims to be Waiheke Island's most-awarded winery. 'Passage Rock has brought Waiheke Syrah to its present-day status and would have to be one of the Auckland region's hottest reds.' These are bold assertions — but they can easily be substantiated.

The flow of top accolades for Passage Rock Reserve Syrah has been relentless. The 2008 vintage won a gold medal at the 2009 Air New Zealand Wine Awards; the 2006 won the Alan Limmer Trophy for Champion Syrah at the 2007 Romeo Bragato Wine Awards. The 2005 vintage set the New Zealand show circuit alight during 2006, scooping four gold medals.

Price: $50

Passage Rock lies at Te Matuku Bay, on the island's south-east coast, far from the main cluster of vineyards further west. David Evans and his wife, Veronika, planted their first vines in 1994 on a sheltered, sunny site, slightly above the estuary.

Passage Rock at first attracted attention for its Cabernet Sauvignon and Merlot-based reds, until Evans fell for Syrah. The variety suits Waiheke Island better than Cabernet Sauvignon, says Evans. 'Every 10 years, we'll have eight good vintages of Syrah, but only four of Cabernet Sauvignon.' Syrah ripens slightly earlier, 'with a better natural balance in the grapes and no "green" characters — you get nice, rich fruit flavours'.

Today, Syrah and Viognier are the two key varieties in Passage Rock's estate vineyard, and they also draw Syrah from sites adjoining the former Peninsula Estate at Oneroa, at the western end of the island.

Evans believes in getting the grapes very ripe. 'The skins are very soft, not raisiny, but flaccid. You are risking the fact that if you get a sudden downpour, they can deteriorate quickly, but we can pick it in a morning.'

Passage Rock Reserve Syrah has long shown the strong influence of new American oak — Evans enjoys a full-on style. However, he is gradually being persuaded of the merits of more subtle French oak, so the 2008 was matured in 'quality, mostly new, French oak barriques'. He describes the 2008 as having 'impressive softness and finesse, while being strong and full-flavoured'.

Passage Rock is also the home of a top-flight, non-reserve Syrah ($35), and a much rarer, dense, Reserve David's Syrah, matured in all-new French oak barriques and priced at $100.

If you like this wine, also try: Passage Rock Syrah; Kennedy Point Waiheke Island Syrah

PENCARROW MARTINBOROUGH PINOT NOIR

PALLISER Estate, Martinborough's largest winery, is also the source of some of its greatest wines. Its size enables it to offer some irresistible bargains under its second-tier label, Pencarrow — especially the Pinot Noir.

'We were probably the first serious producer to put Pinot Noir at $20,' recalled Richard Riddiford, the company's managing director, in *New Zealand Winegrower* in 2010. 'A lot of people who drink wine can't afford to pay $50, $60 or $70 per bottle, but they can afford to pay $20, $25 or $30. So that exposed Pinot Noir to a whole new range of consumers.'

Price: $22

When Pencarrow Pinot Noir 2009 ($22) and Palliser Estate Pinot Noir 2008 ($42) both won gold medals at the 2010 Air New Zealand Wine Awards, Riddiford stated that the gold medal would make no difference to sales of the top label, but would definitely intensify demand for the Pencarrow.

Allan Johnson, Palliser Estate's winemaker for over 20 years, believes Martinborough's climate suits Pinot Noir. 'It's not too hot and not too cold. Compared to Burgundy, we have a longer ripening season but lower temperature peaks, so we get a different fruit expression. The vines have a good balance of foliage and fruit. The rest is Martinborough magic.'

Palliser controls six vineyards in Martinborough, including the 26-hectare Pencarrow vineyard, planted principally in Pinot Noir, and buys grapes from Wairarapa growers and further afield. In some vintages, such as 2008 (when the Martinborough content of the blend was 76 per cent), the wine is labelled as Pencarrow Pinot Noir rather than Pencarrow Martinborough Pinot Noir.

Johnson favours a rich style of Pinot Noir 'with the roast coffee aromas of ripe fruit and good structure'. The Pencarrow red is fermented with natural yeasts and matured for 10 months in French oak casks.

Johnson describes the 2009 vintage as 'displaying lifted aromas of dark cherry, plum and mushroom. The palate is beautifully fruited, showing velvety texture and beautifully integrated, fine tannins. With its supple mouthfeel and excellent fruit intensity, it is already drinking beautifully.'

The 2008 vintage scooped a five-star rating in *Winestate*, proving the Air New Zealand Wine Awards gold for the 2009 was no fluke. Deeply coloured, warm and spicy, rich and full of personality, Pencarrow is clearly one of the best-value Pinot Noirs in the country.

BEST BUY

If you like this wine, also try: Palliser Estate Martinborough Pinot Noir; Villa Maria Cellar Selection Marlborough Pinot Noir

PEREGRINE CENTRAL OTAGO PINOT NOIR

'POWER with elegance' is Greg Hay's goal for Peregrine's most acclaimed wine. 'Those qualities come from Cromwell and Gibbston respectively. We want ripe-fruit characters, without overt oak, and a silky texture.'

Peregrine Central Otago Pinot Noir is a highly seductive red, fresh, richly coloured and beautifully scented. Intensely varietal, it offers strong flavours of cherries, plums, herbs and spices, impressive complexity and a silky-smooth finish. Its instant appeal is enhanced by a slightly lower price than most of its quality peers.

Price: $39

Over the years, the grapes have been sourced from varying sub-regions of Central Otago.

'We source grapes from a minimum of 12 sites throughout the region that allows us to create the wine we feel the consumer wants, rather than be dictated to by the season,' says Hay, who is part-owner of Peregrine and its sales and marketing director.

The key production change over the years has been a shift to markedly lower yields. 'In 1998 and 1999, our crop levels were 7 to 8 tonnes per hectare,' recalls Hay. 'Since 2000, they've been down around 5.5 tonnes per hectare.' The rising standard of the wine also reflects the increasing age of the vines and Peregrine's growing understanding of what each Pinot Noir clone and block provides.

'And we've always had great winemakers,' says Hay. After Peter Bartle's departure in 2010, the production reins are now in the hands of Nadine Cross, previously senior winemaker for Marlborough's Wither Hills.

The 2009 vintage was blended from fruit grown in the Cromwell Basin (85 per cent) and at Gibbston (15 per cent). The grapes were hand-harvested with high sugar levels (23.3 to 25.4 brix), and the wine was matured for 10 months in French oak barrels (27 per cent new).

Peregrine Central Otago Pinot Noir has won a host of top accolades. The 2007 vintage won *Winestate*'s Wine of the Year award in 2009. The first New Zealand wine ever to win the magazine's ultimate prize, it triumphed over 10,000 other contenders.

Then the 2009 scooped the trophy for overall champion of the 2010 Air New Zealand Wine Awards. Peregrine describes the wine as offering 'wonderful flavours of spice, dark cherries, raspberries, and mouth-caressing, silky, fine-grained tannins'.

Under its second-tier brand, Saddleback, Peregrine also makes an enjoyable, drink-young Pinot Noir, typically a floral red with considerable complexity and very good depth of strawberry and spice flavours.

If you like this wine, also try: Saddleback Central Otago Pinot Noir; Felton Road Bannockburn Central Otago Pinot Noir

PURIRI HILLS RESERVE

≫ CLEVEDON, a rural district of South Auckland, just over the water from Waiheke Island, is better known as a playground of the polo set, with their inevitable glasses of Champagne, than for its home-grown, rich red wine. But in Clevedon's lush green valleys, expatriate American Judy Fowler is producing a rivulet of classy blended reds that rank among the country's greatest. 'Nobody *needs* this wine,' admits Fowler. 'My challenge is to make it so good that people *want* to buy it.'

Price: **$70**

Puriri Hills Reserve is a highly distinguished, Merlot-based blend. Deeply coloured, with a generous array of blackcurrant, spice, herb and plum flavours, it is deliciously rich and silky-textured, showing lovely depth and perfume.

A great fan of the scented, velvety reds of St Émilion and Pomerol, in Bordeaux, Fowler planted the first vines in her 2-hectare vineyard at Clevedon in 1997.

Today, the Puriri Hills vineyard, draped over a clay slope overlooking the Wairoa River and Hauraki Gulf, is planted in Merlot, Cabernet Franc, Cabernet Sauvignon, Malbec — and Carmenère. An old Bordeaux variety, now nearly extinct in France but grown widely in Chile, Carmenère was planted as 'Cabernet Franc' — until DNA testing a few years ago revealed its true identity.

Puriri Hills is produced in two models: a lower-priced, Estate bottling and the Reserve, which has a stronger seasoning of new French oak. The grapes are all grown, and the wine is made, on the property. For Puriri Hills Reserve, the *encépagement* (proportion of grape varieties in the blend) in the 2004, 2005 and 2006 vintages has been Merlot (36 to 53 per cent), Carmenère (21 to 46 per cent); and Cabernet Franc (11 to 17 per cent). Cabernet Sauvignon and Malbec are also included in some, but not all, vintages.

The wine is matured in French oak barriques (about 60 per cent new) for 18 to 22 months, bottled without filtering, and then bottle-aged for a year or two, prior to release. A rare red, in recent vintages averaging only 270 cases, it's a delightful mouthful — notably fragrant, dark, lush and velvety.

Puriri Hills also produces another superb red, Pope, named after Ivan Pope, who planted and tended the vines for several years. A blend of Merlot, Carmenère, Cabernet Franc and Malbec, launched from the 2005 vintage, it will be made only in the greatest years — once or twice per decade.

If you like this wine, also try: Alluviale; Te Mata Coleraine

SACRED HILL HELMSMAN CABERNET/MERLOT

AT a London tasting two years ago, attended by several top wine critics, six reds from the Gimblett Gravels were tasted blind alongside six Bordeaux reds. The Cabernet/Merlot and Merlot/Cabernet blends from Hawke's Bay are often described as 'Bordeaux-like', and although the wines are produced on opposite sides of the world, they can be impossible to tell apart.

The UK wine commentators voted Château Lafite-Rothschild 2005 and Château Mouton Rothschild 2005 — both hugely prestigious, sought-after first growths

Price: $65

of the Médoc — into first and second places, followed by Château Angelus 2005, a *premier grand cru classé* of St Émilion. Wedged between the Angelus in third and another famous first-growth, Château Haut-Brion 2005, in fifth, came the big surprise — Sacred Hill Helmsman Cabernet/Merlot 2005.

The four illustrious Bordeaux reds had an average retail price of £660. So what was the UK price of the refined, dark and brambly, densely packed Sacred Hill Helmsman Cabernet/Merlot 2005? £18.

Blended from Cabernet Sauvignon (53 per cent), Merlot (42 per cent) and Cabernet Franc (5 per cent), the 2007 vintage is similar to the 2005 — powerful and deeply coloured, with bold blackcurrant, plum, spice and coffee flavours, complex, firm and long. An authoritative wine, it should flourish in the cellar for a decade. In the US, Harvey Steiman, editor at large of the *Wine Spectator*, gave it 97/100.

A medium-sized winery, Sacred Hill has two joint-venture vineyards, Deerstalkers and Woodlands, in the Gimblett Gravels. The varieties cultivated are all red: Merlot, Cabernet Sauvignon, Cabernet Franc, Malbec and Syrah.

Winemaker Tony Bish sees himself as 'a "vineyard" winemaker, putting into practice the adage that the best wines are made in the vineyard'. He has a 'tremendous belief in the unique attributes of the Gimblett Gravels, as year after year we see wines of intensity, power and finesse emerge from these bony soils'.

Grown in the Deerstalkers Vineyard, the grapes are picked by hand from close-planted, low-yielding vines and the Helmsman Cabernet/Merlot is matured for 18 months in French oak barriques (new and one-year-old).

Bish describes the 2007 as 'deeply coloured, with lifted aromas of sweet leather, together with spicy earth notes, hints of wild mushroom and black liquorice. These aromas follow to a dense, richly fruited palate with excellent depth. [The wine shows] beautiful poise and balance, with supple tannins and a lingering, ripe-fruit aftertaste.' It's a great candidate for the cellar.

If you like this wine, also try: Tom; Te Mata Coleraine

STONYRIDGE LAROSE

>>> SEDUCTIVELY perfumed, with smashing fruit flavours, Stonyridge Larose is a magnificently concentrated Waiheke Island red. It matures superbly for a decade and longer, acquiring savoury leather and tobacco characters and great overall complexity and harmony.

The accolades, local and international, have been many. Oz Clarke, in his *Pocket Wine Book 2005*, described Larose as 'a remarkably Bordeaux-like red of real intensity'. In the U.S., the 2008 vintage was rated 93–95/100 in *The Wine Advocate* (September 2009).

Price: **$90–190**

'Ripeness, smoothness and complexity' are the key qualities Stephen White, the owner, seeks in Larose. 'My original goal was to make a New Zealand red that expresses ripe fruit; so many were so green [herbaceous] when I started. In terms of Bordeaux, I wanted a wine that had some of the strength of Mouton [Château Mouton-Rothschild] and the elegance of [Château] Margaux.'

A crucial factor in his success has been the warm, dry climate of parts of Waiheke Island. 'This valley [Onetangi], this site has an especially good climate. It's north-facing, we have rocks in the ground, and our viticulture is meticulous. We crop the vines lightly [4 tonnes per hectare], and are absolutely dedicated to the idea that wine is made in the vineyard. And we use all five Bordeaux varieties [Cabernet Sauvignon, Merlot, Cabernet Franc, Malbec and Petit Verdot]; five is better than four.'

The vines grow in poor clay soils, threaded with rotten rock, which aids good drainage. A kilometre away lies the sea, 'which means the nights are not too cold; the Bordelaise like that'.

The vinification, says White, is 'pretty low-tech and traditional'. It is matured for a year in oak barriques, predominantly French, but 10 to 20 per cent of the casks are American oak, which he believes adds 'more obvious characters, but also complexity'. The barrels are half new, half one-year-old.

The varietal composition of Larose has changed over the years. The initial vintages were strongly reliant on Cabernet Sauvignon and Merlot (75 per cent), but by 2003 the blend included 43 per cent Malbec and Petit Verdot. Cabernet Sauvignon is now moving back into favour: the 2009 vintage of Larose is 52 per cent Cabernet Sauvignon, supplemented by Malbec (18 per cent), Petit Verdot (15 per cent), Merlot (10 per cent) and Cabernet Franc (5 per cent).

Top vintages of Larose match the intensity and finesse of its model, the great reds of Bordeaux — a rare feat. If you buy it on an *en primeur* basis (payment nine months ahead of delivery), you can save about half of the typical retail price of $190.

If you like this wine, also try: Sacred Hill Helmsman Cabernet/ Merlot; Te Mata Coleraine

STONYRIDGE LUNA NEGRA WAIHEKE ISLAND HILLSIDE MALBEC

THIS is no thin, mean-spirited wine. A supercharged red, overflowing with colour, body and flavour, it's described on the label as 'like doing an energetic salsa with a Cuban beauty queen'.

Malbec-based reds typically impress with their power and exuberant fruitiness, rather than finesse. An old Bordeaux variety, in New Zealand

Price: $80

Malbec is planted principally in Hawke's Bay, but there are plots throughout the upper North Island. It is commonly used as a minority blending partner, adding brilliant colour and a rich fruitiness to its marriages with Merlot, Cabernet Sauvignon and Cabernet Franc. As a straight varietal wine, Malbec can be a bit rustic, but top models can take your breath away with their sheer density and chewy boldness.

Stonyridge, on Waiheke Island, grows Malbec at its Vina del Mar site, near Onetangi Beach. 'Malbec's inherent weakness is that it can overcrop and become diluted and flabby,' the winery reports. 'But our steep, northeast-facing slope and low cropping produces a "Black Moon" Malbec that is thoroughbred.'

The grapes are harvested by hand and during

the ferment the skins are hand-plunged four times daily. After the fermentation has subsided, the wine is held on its skins for another two to four weeks, and then matured for a year in American oak barriques (50 per cent new).

Stonyridge described the 2006 vintage as 'a strongly perfumed wine — berry conserve, black plums, violets, vanilla and spice. The dense palate is packed with ripe berry-fruit flavours . . . [and] well-integrated American oak lends a spicy vanillin aspect. . . . Rich, ripe and decadent.'

In the US, the 2008 Luna Negra scored 91–93 points out of 100 in the highly influential publication *The Wine Advocate* (September 2009). 'There is an attractive herbaceous nose with a touch of vanilla pod, then hints of lavender and violets with very fine definition. Fine tannins on the entry, very good acidity, great focus and poise with bilberry and briary towards the finish, with slight gravelly notes. Lovely.'

Luna Negra couples the full-throttle power of Malbec with the complexity and structure to mature well. In top vintages, with gobs of fruit and layers of blackcurrant, plum, spice, coffee and liquorice flavours, it is deliciously dark and dense.

If you like this wine, also try: Esk Valley The Terraces; Newton Forrest Gimblett Gravels Hawke's Bay Malbec

TE MATA COLERAINE

>>> **NAMED** after the town in Northern Ireland that was the home of founder John Buck's forebears, Coleraine (pronounced Cole-raine, rather than Coler-aine) is one of New Zealand's most prestigious reds, with a pedigree stretching back to the early 1980s. A good vintage Coleraine is a magical wine, with an intensity, complexity and subtlety on the level of a top-class Bordeaux.

Te Mata's highest-profile wine, Coleraine is a deeply flavoured, tightly structured Hawke's Bay Cabernet/Merlot, fragrant and multidimensional.

Price: **$75**

More new oak-influenced than its stablemate, Awatea Cabernets/Merlot, it is more restrained in its youth. Subtlety, concentration and the ability to flourish with cellaring are its hallmarks.

In assembling Coleraine, Buck and winemaker Peter Cowley 'go for a highly concentrated palate; the nose comes later. Coleraine is based on our most concentrated fruit, off our oldest, lowest-cropping vines, grown in the warmest sites.'

The key quality factor, Buck believes, is 'the vineyard site. It's site, site and site — as it is around the world.' The core sites for Coleraine are all in the warm, sheltered Havelock North hills, where the vines' yields are restricted to an average of only 7.5 tonnes of grapes per hectare.

Although based mainly on Cabernet Sauvignon (which forms 50–55 per cent of the blend), Coleraine is a blend of three classic Bordeaux varieties, with 30–40 per cent Merlot and 5–20 per cent Cabernet Franc. 'A straight Cabernet Sauvignon is not as good as one that's blended with Merlot to fill out the middle palate,' says Cowley, 'and we use Cabernet Franc to add charm and red-berry fragrance.' The wine is matured for 20 months in French oak barriques (predominantly new).

A complete vertical tasting of Coleraine (1982 to 2006), held in mid-2008, showed that all vintages since 1989 were still drinking well and the 2004 to 2006 vintages had scaled new heights (surpassing the great trio of 1989–91).

Te Mata views the 2009 vintage as the best ever. 'Coleraine '09 has a saturated magenta colour with concentrated aromas of blackcurrants, spice and dark, old-fashioned roses. The palate opens with the dense, sweet, dark berry fruits indicative of a great year. The focus quickly turns to rich, fine tannins that fill the mouth, leaving a lasting impression.'

Breed, rather than brute power, is the signature of Coleraine, New Zealand's closest parallel to great Bordeaux.

If you like this wine, also try: Stonyridge Larose; Sacred Hill Helmsman Cabernet/Merlot

TE MATA WOODTHORPE VINEYARD MERLOT/ CABERNETS

TE Mata Estate's Woodthorpe Vineyard range — Chardonnay, Sauvignon Blanc, Gamay Noir, Syrah and Merlot/Cabernets — offers five single-vineyard wines of eye-catching quality and value. Their broad appeal is summed up by Te Mata's own description: 'everyday luxury'.

Given Te Mata Estate's track record, now spanning 30 years, of producing distinguished claret-style reds in Hawke's Bay, you'd expect its third-tier label to be a decent drop. Te Mata Woodthorpe Vineyard Merlot/Cabernets, the company's biggest-selling wine, is a Bordeaux-like red with good ripeness, density and complexity — yet widely available for less than $20.

Price: $19

Why is it so popular? Te Mata points to its accessible, ripe-fruit flavours, combined with an elegant palate structure. The winery is a 'leading producer of Cabernet/Merlot blends, a reputation founded since 1982 upon the excellence of our flagship wine, Coleraine. The same quality grapegrowing and winemaking applies to Woodthorpe Merlot/Cabernets.'

Woodthorpe Vineyard lies 14 kilometres inland, near the Tutaekuri River, on the south side of the Dartmoor Valley. Named after its first European owner, O.L.W. (Woodthorpe) Bousefield, the property was acquired by Te Mata in 1993. Since then, 75 hectares of vines have fanned out over its north-facing terraces. The key varieties planted in free-draining, light, volcanic soils with a gravelly base are Chardonnay, Sauvignon Blanc and Merlot, with smaller plots of Cabernet Franc, Cabernet Sauvignon, Viognier, Syrah, Gamay Noir and Petit Verdot.

Woodthorpe Vineyard Merlot/Cabernets is a blend of four varieties. Merlot accounts for about 45 per cent of the blend, followed by Cabernet Sauvignon and Cabernet Franc (together, around 40 per cent of the total) and Petit Verdot (15 per cent). The wine is matured for 15 to 17 months in French oak barrels (new and seasoned).

Te Mata Estate describes the 2008 vintage as displaying 'a deep, red garnet colour with warm [ripe] aromas of spicy cherry, boysenberry and dark plum. Dark cherry syrup, cedar and chocolate all feature on the palate, with firm, velvety tannins and a touch of liquorice on the long finish.'

Woodthorpe Vineyard Merlot/Cabernets always reminds me of a good, minor Bordeaux, with very satisfying depth of fresh, berryish fruit flavours, some savoury, spicy complexity — and great drinkability.

BEST BUY

If you like this wine, also try: Te Mata Awatea Cabernets/ Merlot; Church Road Hawke's Bay Merlot/Cabernet Sauvignon

TERRAVIN HILLSIDE RESERVE MARLBOROUGH PINOT NOIR

>>>

MIKE Eaton, a vastly experienced Marlborough viticulturist who has also worked in three French wine regions — Burgundy, Pouilly-sur-Loire and the Jura — is a great fan of slopes. 'Hillside vineyards have hotter days and cooler nights,' he told *Cuisine*, 'which give the best of both worlds. A north-facing hillside vineyard will produce better wine, but it will also produce a wine that is unique, thanks to the wide range of aspects and soils on a sloping site.'

Price: **$56**

- -

Terravin Hillside Reserve is one of Marlborough's greatest reds. A powerful yet supple Pinot Noir, it is notably generous, rich and opulent, in a deliciously sweet-fruited and complex style.

The Clayvin Vineyard in the Brancott Valley, today the source of one of Fromm's finest reds, was originally owned and planted by Eaton. He describes it as 'the first hillside vineyard in Marlborough'. After selling the grapes to the winery for several years, he sold Fromm the vineyard too.

Resuming the search for land, he found his perfect Pinot Noir site in the Omaka Valley.

Ranging from 105 to 160 metres above sea level, it is north-facing and steeply sloping (12 to 17 degrees), with clay-bound soils. From his 4-hectare vineyard, each year Eaton produces about 800 cases of Pinot Noir.

Eaton has been deeply inspired by Burgundy, where he discovered a 'harmony of fruit and *terroir* that fully reflects the village appellation and the grower himself. While the world homogenises itself in a lake of perfectly made, pure fruit bombs that have the individuality of Coca-Cola . . . it is this desire to be individual and true to the land that will see Burgundy live on.'

The grapes for the Hillside Reserve Pinot Noir (until recently labelled Hillside Selection) are harvested by hand from the centre of the slope at an advanced stage of ripeness (24 to 25.5 brix), and the juice is fermented with natural yeasts. After maturation for 16 to 20 months in French oak barriques (40 to 70 per cent new), the wine is bottled without fining or filtering.

Packed with personality, Terravin Hillside Reserve Pinot Noir is a magnificent red, arrestingly savoury and dense.

If you like this wine, also try: Terravin Pinot Noir; Fromm Clayvin Vineyard Marlborough Pinot Noir

TOM

'THE finest red wine ever in New Zealand' is how Montana — now Pernod Ricard NZ — in 1997 promoted the debut 1995 vintage of Tom. At $100, Tom ranks among the country's most expensive reds.

'Tom' honours Tom McDonald, the first modern-era winemaker to chart Hawke's Bay's red-wine potential and the driving force behind its first prestige red, McWilliam's Cabernet Sauvignon. Two years after McDonald's death in 1987, Montana bought and rejuvenated his old winery at Taradale

Price: $100

— now called Church Road Winery — and later engaged the Bordeaux house of Cordier to help upgrade its red wines.

The stylish 1991 vintage of Church Road Cabernet Sauvignon/Merlot was the first fruit of the Montana/Cordier link, followed in 1994 by its big brother, Church Road Reserve Cabernet Sauvignon/ Merlot — and in 1995 by Tom.

A blend of varying proportions of Cabernet Sauvignon and Merlot, matured in French oak barriques, Tom is notably complex and harmonious. Savoury, earthy and spicy, it is very different in style to the fresh, fruit-driven reds so often produced in the New World.

A Love Affair with Wine, published in 2007 to relate the Church Road story, says that for Tom, 'the Church Road winemakers walk each row and mark the lowest vigour areas to guide the hand-picking team. . . . Each tank is tasted on a daily basis. . . . Once off skins, the wine is filled to predominantly new French oak [where it] remains for up to 22 months.'

The 2007 Tom, grown in the Gimblett Gravels, is a blend of Cabernet Sauvignon (51 per cent) and Merlot (49 per cent). Fermented in a French oak *cuve* (vat) and a conventional, closed-top, stainless steel fermenter, the batches were matured for 15 months in French oak barriques (71 per cent new), blended, returned to barrel for a further six months' maturation, and then bottled without fining or filtration.

Church Road describes the wine as offering 'a complex array of black fruits, floral notes and secondary complexities, including cedar, cigar box, earth, spice and dark chocolate. In the tradition of great Bordeaux wines, Tom 2007 exhibits exceptional concentration balanced by a backbone of firm tannin. . . . This is a dense, multidimensional wine that changes and unfolds with time in the glass.'

Designed as a 'food' wine, Tom is not a blockbuster, but shows rare finesse — a densely packed, savoury red, with fine-grained tannins and rich, lasting flavour.

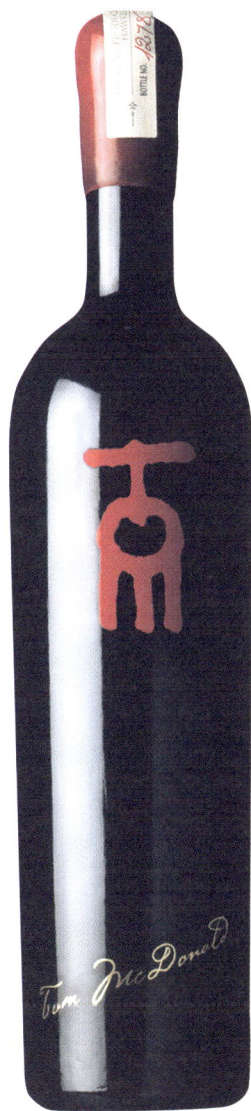

If you like this wine, also try: Te Mata Coleraine; Church Road Reserve Hawke's Bay Cabernet/Merlot

TRINITY HILL GIMBLETT GRAVELS TEMPRANILLO

'SICK of writing the notes for this wine,' admitted Steve Smith, chairman of judges at the 2010 Air New Zealand Wine Awards, 'because it wins all the time.' The 2008 vintage of Trinity Hill Gimblett Gravels Tempranillo won the trophy for Champion Other Red Styles — as it did in 2009.

At the same show in 2008, the 2007 vintage won the trophy; in 2007, the

Price: $35

trophy was not awarded; in 2006, the 2005 . . . you guessed it. From one vintage to the next, this is a classy red, full of personality. Deeply coloured, it is savoury and complex, with generous plum and spice flavours, finely balanced and lasting.

John Hancock, a South Australian winemaker who arrived in New Zealand in 1979 and co-founded Trinity Hill in 1993, constantly experiments with unfamiliar grape varieties. 'Not so much for the sake of being different,' he told *New Zealand Winegrower*, 'but purely because we are such a young, new wine-producing nation.'

The classic grape of Rioja, Tempranillo is widely planted in northern and central Spain. It is prized for its strawberry, spice and tobacco-flavoured wines, capable of maturing gracefully for many years.

Hancock first encountered the variety under its Portuguese name, Tinta Roriz, when he worked at Morton Estate, in the Bay of Plenty. Today, in the Gimblett Gravels, he finds Tempranillo to be an early ripener (*temprano* is Spanish for 'early'), giving it a distinct advantage over such late-ripeners as Cabernet Sauvignon.

To produce a 'complete' wine, Tempranillo grown in Hawke's Bay needs to be blended, Hancock believes. The key partner in the blend so far (about 10 per cent of the finished wine) has been Touriga Nacional, a top Portuguese variety known for its concentrated flavours and high tannin levels. Much later-ripening, Touriga Nacional adds 'depth, weight and complexity'. The 2008 vintage also included splashes of Malbec and Viognier.

The grapes are picked by hand and the wine is matured for up to a year in a mix of tanks and French (90 per cent) and American oak barriques (25 per cent new).

Rich, ripe and instantly inviting, Trinity Hill Gimblett Gravels Tempranillo is a satisfying red with excellent complexity and density. It's a rare panel that doesn't vote it straight into the five-star category.

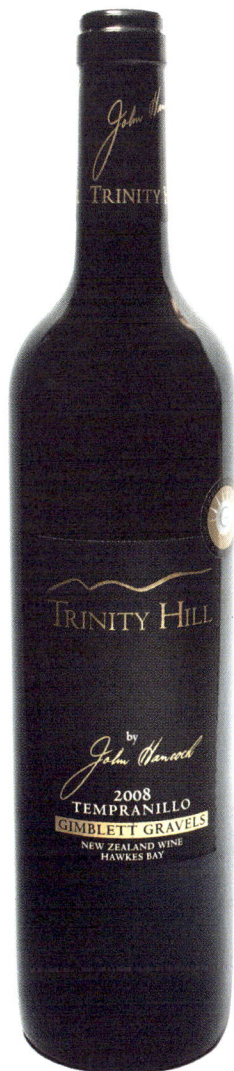

If you like this wine, also try: Black Barn Hawke's Bay Tempranillo; Trinity Hill The Gimblett

〈〈〈

TRINITY HILL THE GIMBLETT

'THE Gimblett' is the top claret-style red from one of Hawke's Bay's best producers, with a deep stake in the Gimblett Gravels. The early 2002 and 2004 vintages, labelled 'Trinity Hill Homage The Gimblett', were priced around $100, but since 2005 this Merlot-based blend has offered spectacular value at $30 to $35.

Dense and age-worthy, the 2008 vintage offers rich blackcurrant and spice flavours, firm, layered and long. The 2005 won a gold medal and trophy for the best Merlot-dominant blend at the 2007 Hawke's Bay A & P Mercedes-Benz Wine Awards, a performance repeated by the 2006 vintage in 2008. The 2008 vintage collected a gold medal at the 2010 New Zealand International Wine Show.

Price: $34

The grapes are grown in the Gimblett Estate, Stockbridge and Tin Shed vineyards in the Gimblett Gravels. The shingly soils 'are extremely free-draining and of low fertility,' reports Trinity Hill, 'growing low-vigour vines producing small crops of intensely coloured and flavoured grapes.' The vines are shoot-thinned before flowering, crop-thinned just before *veraison* (the start of the final stage of ripening), and later bunch-thinned, to achieve low yields of 6 to 7 tonnes of grapes per hectare.

Merlot is the crucial ingredient in the varietal recipe, ranging from 41 to 61 per cent, but Cabernet Sauvignon (2 per cent in 2005, 43 per cent in 2008) can be important too. The other grapes are Petit Verdot (up to 15 per cent), Cabernet Franc (up to 11 per cent), and Malbec (up to 21 per cent). These figures reflect the 2005 to 2008 vintages. The grapes are picked by hand and the wine is matured for 18 to 20 months in principally French oak barrels, 40 per cent new.

Trinity Hill describes The Gimblett 2008 as 'a wine of power, elegance and complexity. The beautiful rich red colour and the black fruit aromas and flavours are complemented by a soft, mouthfilling structure and a fine-grained texture.' It's a notably rich wine, bargain-priced.

For those with tighter purse-strings, Trinity Hill also produces a good-value, claret-style red, The Trinity. Matured mostly in seasoned French oak casks and finely balanced for easy drinking, it also includes a splash of Syrah.

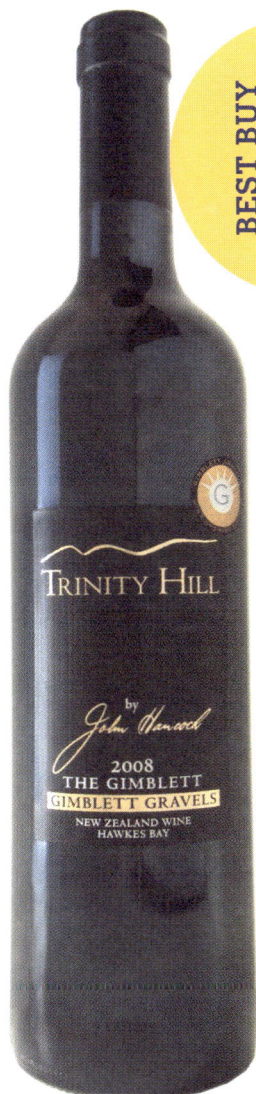

BEST BUY

If you like this wine, also try: Clearview Enigma; Church Road Hawke's Bay Merlot/Cabernet Sauvignon

VIDAL HAWKE'S BAY MERLOT/CABERNET SAUVIGNON

THIS moderately priced, $20 red is a star of the show circuit, showing what exceptional value the wines of big companies — Vidal is an integral part of the Villa Maria empire — can deliver. For instance, the 2008 vintage won a gold medal at the 2010 Royal Easter Show Wine Awards and a five-star rating from *Cuisine* (September 2010), which also ranked it as 'Top New Zealand Merlot'.

Price: **$20**

At its best, Vidal Hawke's Bay Merlot/Cabernet Sauvignon is a very elegant, Bordeaux-like wine with rich blackcurrant, plum, spice and nut flavours, fresh and long. The new oak influence is more restrained than in its higher-priced stablemate, Vidal Reserve Hawke's Bay Merlot/Cabernet Sauvignon, but that helps to give the wine great drinkability in its youth.

During the 1960s, Vidal Wines — then run by Frank, Cecil and Leslie Vidal, whose father, Anthony, founded the company in 1905 — enjoyed a solid reputation for its 'Claret' and 'Burgundy'. Later, acclaimed winemakers such as Kate Radburnd (now at C.J. Pask) and Rod McDonald set the red-wine standard far higher. Hugh Crichton, appointed Vidal winemaker in 2006, had earlier made wine in

Central Otago, Gisborne, Italy — and Bordeaux.

Vidal's grapes are drawn from company-owned vineyards and contract growers around Hawke's Bay. The fruit for the Merlot/Cabernet Sauvignon is grown principally in the Gimblett Gravels. Merlot dominates the blend. For the 2007, 2008 and 2009 vintages, Merlot accounted for 46 per cent to 68 per cent of the wine, ahead of Cabernet Sauvignon (17 per cent to 39 per cent), Malbec (3 per cent to 11 per cent), and Cabernet Franc (zero to 12 per cent).

Maturation has typically been in French and American oak barrels, for up to 15 months. However, the 2009 vintage brought a move to a more 'fruit-driven' style, with 40 per cent of the wine held in tanks, and 60 per cent barrel-aged for a year, before final blending and bottling.

Crichton describes the 2008 vintage as offering 'aromas of red fruits and spice. Bursting with rich black plum, cassis and cedar, the palate's long, smooth finish is supported by supple tannins.'

Full-bodied, with deep blackcurrant, plum and spice flavours, finely integrated oak and a silky-smooth finish, at $20 this deliciously rich, rounded red is a steal.

BEST BUY

If you like this wine, also try: Church Road Hawke's Bay Merlot/Cabernet Sauvignon; Craggy Range Gimblett Gravels Vineyard Merlot

VILLA MARIA CELLAR SELECTION HAWKE'S BAY MERLOT/ CABERNET SAUVIGNON

THE 2000 and 2002 vintages scooped Best Buy of the Year awards in my annual *Buyer's Guide to New Zealand Wines,* so it's no surprise Villa Maria's mid-priced Hawke's Bay red features in this book. It offers superb value.

Price: **$23**

The accolades keep rolling in. The 2007 vintage won three gold medals in New Zealand; the 2008 collected a gold medal at the 2010 Hawke's Bay A & P Mercedes-Benz Wine Awards; the 2009 vintage captured a gold medal at the Royal Easter Show Wine Awards in 2011. That's impressive for a large-volume wine, readily available for less than $25.

A dark, strapping red, it's an 'upfront' style with dense blackcurrant and spice flavours, a hint of fruit cake, and firm tannins. If you like bold, flavour-packed reds, don't miss it.

The grapes are grown mostly in the company's Omahu Gravels, Ngakirikiri and Twyford Gravels vineyards, in the Gimblett Gravels, where the warmth and free-draining, stony soils 'encourage devigorated vines and low yields'. Merlot is the major variety, during the 2007 to 2009 vintages accounting for

47 per cent to 64 per cent of the blend, followed by Cabernet Sauvignon (26 per cent to 42 per cent), and Malbec (2 per cent to 10 per cent).

The wine is matured for 18 months in French, American and Hungarian barriques (about 40 per cent new). Villa Maria describes the 2009 vintage as a 'dark and deeply fragrant wine [in which] layers of berry and plum flavours combine with complex cedar and savoury characters'.

Compared to Villa Maria's Reserve reds, sold at over twice the price, the Cellar Selection is based on slightly heavier-cropping vines and is aged in a lower proportion of new oak barrels. 'The tannins tend to be a bit softer, so it's more enjoyable in its youth,' says Alistair Maling, group winemaker for Villa Maria.

Given the surging popularity of Pinot Noir in New Zealand, are Bordeaux-style reds such as the Cellar Selection underrated by many wine lovers? Maling believes so. 'In our export markets, we get the best response in the UK. They really understand Bordeaux-style reds there.'

If you are a Merlot fan, Villa Maria produces several other reds of high interest, notably a modestly priced Private Bin Hawke's Bay Merlot, Merlot [Organic] and Merlot/Cabernet Sauvignon; a Cellar Selection Hawke's Bay Merlot [Organic]; and an arrestingly dark and dense, multi-layered Reserve Hawke's Bay Merlot.

BEST BUY

If you like this wine, also try: Vidal Hawke's Bay Merlot/ Cabernet Sauvignon; Church Road Hawke's Bay Merlot/Cabernet Sauvignon

VILLA MARIA CELLAR SELECTION MARLBOROUGH PINOT NOIR

VILLA Maria produces at least 10 Pinot Noirs: a Reserve and four Single Vineyard reds, all from Marlborough; two Private Bin models, grown in Marlborough and Central Otago; two Marlborough and one Hawke's Bay-grown bottlings from its subsidiary companies, Vidal and Esk Valley — and this great-value label.

Price: **$32**

Finesse and gracefulness are the key attributes of the Cellar Selection Pinot Noir. Ruby-hued, with an enticing bouquet of cherries and plums, gently seasoned with oak, it is harmonious, with delicious depth of ripe sweet-fruit flavours, fine, supple tannins and enormous charm.

The Cellar Selection is effectively Villa Maria's middle-tier Pinot Noir, positioned below its much higher-priced Reserve and Single Vineyard wines, but above the Private Bin reds. For a wine that can often be snapped up for $25 or less, it is exceptionally good, with a glowing track record in competitions. The 2007 vintage won three gold medals in Australia, plus the trophy for champion Pinot Noir at the 2008 National Wine Show of

Australia; the 2008 vintage won the Pinot Noir trophy at the 2010 International Cool Climate Wine Show; and the 2009 was awarded a gold medal at the 2010 Air New Zealand Wine Awards.

Villa Maria attributes its success with Pinot Noir to its fundamental belief that 'quality wine starts with quality fruit'. Achieving ripe, disease-free grapes is crucial; so is cropping the vines lightly.

Once at the winery, the hand-picked grapes are treated 'with the aim of over-delivering'. During rigorous tastings at the blending stage, any wine that fails to meet the desired quality standard is relegated to a lower-priced label.

Villa Maria Cellar Selection Marlborough Pinot Noir is blended from grapes grown in the Awatere and Wairau valleys. The juice is fermented with natural and cultured yeasts, and the wine is matured for nine months in French oak barriques (18 per cent new in 2009).

Villa Maria's winemakers describe the 2009 vintage as 'concentrated and rich, displaying long layers of flavour, subtle wild thyme notes, integrated acidity and fine, grainy tannins. An elegant Pinot Noir, exhibiting finesse and complexity, with underlying structure and a silky texture.'

In top vintages, this perfumed, vibrantly fruity, rich and flowing red is arguably the best-value Pinot Noir in the country.

If you like this wine, also try: Dog Point Vineyard Marlborough Pinot Noir; Peregrine Central Otago Pinot Noir

VARIETY INDEX

WINE BRAND INDEX